AT THE

Table

WITH

Jesus

Also by Louie Giglio

Don't Give the Enemy a Seat at Your Table

Never Too Far

Not Forsaken

Goliath Must Fall

The Comeback

Waiting Here for You

Indescribable

I Am Not but I Know I Am

The Air I Breathe

Children's Books

Goliath Must Fall for Young Readers

How Great Is Our God: 100 Indescribable Devotions About God & Science

Indescribable: 100 Devotions About God & Science

Indescribable for Little Ones

The Wonder of Creation: 100 More Devotions About God & Science

AT THE

Table

WITH

Jesus

66 DAYS TO DRAW CLOSER TO CHRIST
AND FORTIFY YOUR FAITH

LOUIE GIGLIO

 passionpublishing

W PUBLISHING GROUP

AN IMPRINT OF THOMAS NELSON

Published in Nashville, Tennessee, by W Publishing, an imprint of Thomas Nelson.

Thomas Nelson titles may be purchased in bulk for educational, business, fundraising, or sales promotional use. For information, please email SpecialMarkets@ThomasNelson.com.

Any internet addresses, phone numbers, or company or product information printed in this book are offered as a resource and are not intended in any way to be or to imply an endorsement by Thomas Nelson, nor does Thomas Nelson vouch for the existence, content, or services of these sites, phone numbers, companies, or products beyond the life of this book.

ISBN 978-0-7852-5612-0 (audiobook)
ISBN 978-0-7852-5611-3 (eBook)
ISBN 978-0-7852-5610-6 (TP)

Library of Congress Cataloging-in-Publication Data

Library of Congress Control Number: 2021938862

Printed in the United States of America

23 24 25 26 27 LBC 8 7 6 5 4

Contents

Section 4: Jesus Is Our Teacher

Section 5: Jesus Is Our Great I Am

Section 6: Jesus Is Lord of All

Section 7: Jesus Is Our Friend

Contents

viii

Introduction

Have you ever wondered what the world's most expensive table might be like? Me neither. But I saw a headline of an article recently that caught my attention, and, of course, I ended up reading the whole thing.

Turns out the world's most expensive table is called the Tufft pier table, named after the guy who built it: Thomas Tufft. (Imagine what a good marketer could do if Thomas were in business today. *Built Tufft!*) Crafted in 1776, this table was sold to a general store owner from Lumberton, New Jersey, named Richard Edwards. All that sounds pretty normal, right?

Now comes the crazy part. A little more than two hundred years later, one of Edwards's descendants sold that same table at a Christie's auction for $4.6 million! Here's how the *New York Times* reported on the sale:

> The prize of the sale was a Philadelphia console or pier table with a Chinese-style apron of pierced fretwork, tall legs, narrow ankles and finely detailed ball-and-claw feet. The rococo rarity, carved by Thomas Tufft in 1775–76, was sold for $4.6 million on Jan. 20, becoming the most expensive table in the world. The price was well above the presale estimate of at most $1.5 million.[1]

When I first read that, I thought, *Umm, okay. How do narrow ankles translate to four-and-a-half million bucks?*

I mean, what is more commonplace in the world today than a table? Everybody has one. More than one, probably. Our homes are packed with them, from dinner tables to breakfast nooks to end tables to bedside tables to coffee tables. Go to most parks and you'll find a whole line of picnic tables sitting out there on the grass, free for anyone to use. Or just throw a piece of plywood on top of some cinderblocks, and *boom!* there's a table.

And yet . . .

The more I think about it, the more I realize tables have a symbolic value within our culture. Tables are connected to some of the most important and meaningful moments of our lives.

When we're at home, for example, we gather around a table with those nearest and dearest to us. We have first dates at tables. We celebrate golden anniversaries at tables. We forge new friendships at tables. We teach our kids important lessons at tables. We even make business deals by shaking hands over and signing papers on conference room tables.

In a lot of ways, then, a table is an icon of influence. Of access. When you let someone join you at a table, you're inviting them in. Bringing them close. Opening yourself in a way that's vulnerable.

So, yeah, I guess I can see why tables are valuable. Does that mean I'm going to break the bank the next time I need some new dining room furniture? In a word, nope. But I do want you to consider the importance of the table in your own life. Specifically, what I call the table of your mind.

Recently I wrote a book called *Don't Give the Enemy a Seat at Your Table*. It was inspired in part by Psalm 23:5, which says, "You prepare a table before me in the presence of my enemies." I love the imagery of that verse. In my mind's eye, I see a green field where my enemies are prowling around, looking for a way to destroy me. Yet right there—right in the middle of the wolves and the hyenas—I see the Good Shepherd setting up a table and inviting me over. I don't have to worry when I sit down at that table. I don't have to protect myself or say anything to justify myself against my foes. Why? Because I'm at the table with the King of the Universe.

Unfortunately, it's been my observation that many people, myself included, have a terrible habit of pulling out a chair and gesturing to those ravenous wolves prowling around the perimeter: *Come on over. Have a seat.* We open ourselves to the Enemy. We give Satan access to our minds and our hearts.

Don't Give the Enemy a Seat at Your Table is my call for all followers of God to take back our tables. To stand up in our Christ-given authority and rid ourselves of negative influences. To shut our doors against the lies, the doubts, and the fears Satan whispers so consistently and so persistently after he weasels his way into our space.

Ridding ourselves of negative influences is a critical step in winning the battle for our own hearts and minds. If you haven't had the chance to read *Don't Give the Enemy a Seat at Your Table*, you may find it helpful alongside this sixty-six-day journey.

My goal for this book is to give you the next necessary step. Because once you've removed what's harmful from your table, you need to actively open some space for what is most helpful—and there is nothing more helpful in your life and mine than a genuine, thriving relationship with Jesus Christ.

At the Table with Jesus is an invitation to do just what the title suggests: to sit down with Jesus at the table of your mind. To give Him access and influence in the deepest way possible. To fully trust that He is good and that He alone has your best interest at heart.

What does that look like? I'm reminded of Proverbs 18:10: "The name of the LORD is a fortified tower; the righteous run to it and are safe." In my mind, I still see the same green field. I still see the table God has prepared for me in the midst of my enemies. But now there's something new, something powerful and protective. Now I see a fortified tower built around and above that table. Can you see it too? Huge cut stones, stacked and cemented. A rising wall on all four sides. Impenetrable.

That fortified tower is created by the presence of Jesus at your table. He is the One we run to when we need to find safety. Security. Fulfillment. Purpose. He is the One who fortifies our minds against the attacks of the Enemy.

Over these next sixty-six days, we are going to explore eleven foundational truths about who Jesus is, curated to help you know Him better as you invite Him closer. Jesus is God. He is human. He is our Savior. He is a Rabbi, a teacher. Jesus is I AM. He is Lord. He is our friend. He is Head of the church and our great High Priest. Jesus is the Lamb of God. And Jesus is King.

You could think of each of these truths as a block in the fortified tower surrounding your mind and your heart. It's my sincere hope you will develop a deeper connection with Jesus during this journey. I hope you will find greater confidence in Christ as your strong tower. And I hope you will take advantage of this opportunity to saturate yourself in Christ—to soak in the truth of who He is, what He values, and how He is working—so you can live with confidence and clarity as His disciple.

You've listened to the Enemy long enough. You've listened to the culture long enough. You've listened to the news media and the entertainment media and social media long enough. It's time to sit down at the table with Christ and fortify your faith with truth. And it's time to take that next step toward the life you were always created to live.

Jesus Is God

DAY 1

Jesus Is God

"You are not yet fifty years old," they said to him, "and you have seen Abraham!"

"Very truly I tell you," Jesus answered, "before Abraham was born, I am!" At this, they picked up stones to stone him, but Jesus hid himself, slipping away from the temple grounds.

JOHN 8:57–59

There have been many bold statements in human history. Patrick Henry declaring "Give me liberty or give me death!" is a good example. So is Harriet Tubman's exhortation to the slaves she led through the Underground Railroad: "If you hear the dogs, keep going. If you see the torches in the woods, keep going. If there's shouting after you, keep going. Don't ever stop. Keep going. If you want a taste of freedom, keep going."[1]

Yet Jesus claiming to be God is without a doubt the boldest statement ever made or recorded.

And, yes, that is exactly what Jesus claimed in the Scripture passage above. A couple of thousand years before Jesus walked the streets of Jerusalem, God spoke to Moses through a burning bush. When Moses humbly asked to know God's name, "God said to Moses, 'I AM WHO I AM.' And He said, 'Thus you shall say to the children of Israel, "I AM has sent me to you"'" (Ex. 3:14 NKJV).

Back in those Jerusalem streets, there was a different group of people asking the questions, this time not so humbly. The religious leaders wanted to know who Jesus thought He was. In fact, they demanded to know. And when Jesus mentioned a connection between Himself and Abraham, they scoffed. Abraham was a national treasure for the Jewish people. A founding father. One of the most respected personages in history, right up there with Moses. *What on earth could this rabbi be talking about?*

That's when Jesus dropped the bomb: "Before Abraham was, I AM."

This is Day 1 of our journey together, and the very first thing you need to process and understand is that Jesus is God. *The* God. The one and only Creator and Sustainer of the universe. And this same God has prepared a table for you in the presence of your enemies. This same God—the one and only God—has invited you to join Him. Jesus is God, and He is inviting you close.

It's worth chewing on the truth of Jesus' divinity for a few moments. Jesus is not just an ambassador for God. Jesus is not just part of God. Jesus is not just someone who lived a good life and taught some helpful things and deserves to be remembered favorably by history because He helped us find a better understanding of God.

No, Jesus is God. Full stop.

The religious leaders who were listening to Jesus understood His claim, even if they didn't accept it. That's why they picked up stones. In their minds, they were obeying what God commanded in His law: "Whoever blasphemes the name of the LORD shall surely be put to death. All the congregation shall certainly stone him" (Lev. 24:16 NKJV). They were zealous in their religion even as they missed the Author of their faith.

I encourage you not to repeat their mistake. Instead, as you take a step closer to Christ at the table of your mind, I hope you'll bow in His presence and declare for all to hear, "Lord Jesus Christ, You are God, and I worship You."

Response

What risks are you taking when you acknowledge the truth that Jesus is God?

What rewards will you receive by making that confession?

> **SCRIPTURE MEMORY**
>
> If anyone acknowledges that Jesus is the Son of God, God lives in them and they in God.
>
> **—1 JOHN 4:15**

DAY 2

Jesus Is the Son of God

"But what about you?" [Jesus] asked. "Who do you say I
am?"

Simon Peter answered, "You are the Messiah, the Son of
the living God."

Jesus replied, "Blessed are you, Simon son of Jonah, for
this was not revealed to you by flesh and blood, but by my
Father in heaven."

MATTHEW 16:15-17

All the best superheroes have secret identities. Bruce Wayne throws
on a costume and becomes Batman. Carol Danvers transforms into
Captain Marvel. Diana Prince grabs her lasso and fights crime as
Wonder Woman. And all Clark Kent has to do is run into a phone
booth and take off his glasses to become Superman.

Jesus had His own secret identity of sorts. The people of Galilee
knew Him as a carpenter, the son of Joseph. For thirty years they
watched Him play as a child, apprentice with Joseph, and build their
homes. Then, seemingly out of the blue, Jesus launched a ministry. He
taught in the synagogue. He started traveling and taking on disciples,
fulfilling the profile of a rabbi. Then He began healing the sick and
casting out demons—even raising the dead.

Everywhere Jesus went, the same question rang out over and over
again: *Who are you?* The people wanted to know. The religious leaders
wanted to know. Even the Romans wanted to know.

Of course, some people already knew. Well, not exactly *people*.

When Jesus healed a demon-possessed man in the region of the Gadarenes, the outgoing demon tried to blow the lid on Jesus' secret identity: "What do you want with me, Jesus, Son of the Most High God? In God's name don't torture me!" (Mark 5:7). When Jesus was tempted by Satan in the wilderness, the ancient serpent tacitly acknowledged Jesus' superhero status: "The tempter came to him and said, 'If you are the Son of God, tell these stones to become bread'" (Matt. 4:3).

Eventually it was Peter—brash, impulsive, overzealous Peter—who clued in the rest of the disciples when he told Jesus, "You are the Messiah, the Son of the living God."

Yes, Jesus is the Son of God. But what does that actually mean? Obviously Jesus isn't merely a son in a biological sense. He has always existed, and as we already saw in Day 1, Jesus *is* God. So how should we understand His title as the Son *of* God?

The answer lies in the culture of the ancient world. In that time, each father was the patriarch of his family. He carried all the authority, managed all the resources, and commanded all the respect. However, it was understood that the role of patriarch would eventually be transferred to his firstborn son. Therefore, that son often served as a representative of his father. If the patriarch needed to purchase something, for example, he might send his son to finalize the deal. The son would take up his father's authority and go out in his name.

That's how Jesus operated in our world. He is equal to the Father, but He came as a representative of the Father. He came with the Father's authority and had access to the Father's resources in order to accomplish the Father's work. And so He is rightly known as the Son of God.

Jesus is more significant than any superhero—way more. But He's also closer than any comic-book character could ever be. The Son of God has stepped down into your world and offered to strengthen you, to fortify your mind and heart. How will you respond?

Response

The apostle John declared that those who follow Jesus are "children of God." How should we understand that phrase?

What are ways we can acknowledge Jesus' proper status, as Peter did?

SCRIPTURE MEMORY

If anyone acknowledges that Jesus is the Son of God, God lives in them and they in God.

—1 JOHN 4:15

Jesus Is the Word of God

In the beginning was the Word, and the Word was with God, and the Word was God. He was with God in the beginning.
JOHN 1:1-2

How many Bibles exist out there in the world? The answer is a lot. Way more than anyone could count or keep track of. That's because the Bible is not only the bestselling book in history, but it is continually the bestselling book in the present. In fact, there are more than 100 million Bibles sold or given away every year.[1] That's nearly 275,000 every day. And that doesn't even take into account digital versions of the Word.

Next question: Have you ever wondered what the Bible *is*? What it really is?

It's easy to think of the Bible—God's Word—as a book. Or, more accurately, a collection of books. Something that can be sold or given away. But it's more than that. And we can get a glimpse of what that looks like when we read the first verse of John's Gospel: "In the beginning was the Word, and the Word was with God, and the Word was God."

John was talking about Jesus in that verse. That's why he used "He" at the beginning of verse 2. Jesus is the Word of God who was "with God" at the beginning and is God.

There are two ways to understand this connection between Jesus and "the Word."

The first is what we call *revelation*. The Bible is God's specific revelation to humanity. It's one of the primary ways God has revealed Himself to us. Who He is, what He does, what He values, and so on. Jesus is the other primary way God has revealed Himself to us. As John said later in his gospel, "The Word became flesh and made his dwelling among us" (1:14). Jesus revealed God to us not through lines on a page but by living, breathing, walking, talking, healing, teaching, and correcting.

The second way to understand Jesus as the Word of God goes a little deeper into the historical context of John's day. In the ancient world, philosophers used the word *logos* to describe the concept of speaking or thinking. On a broad level, they referred to the *logos* as reason itself, as the mind of God.

Well, the word *Logos* is what John used to describe Jesus in these verses. "In the beginning was the Logos . . ." John wanted to introduce Jesus to his readers by pointing out that Jesus is unique. Unprecedented. Divine. He was and is the mind of God personified. The Logos made flesh.

In short, Jesus is the Word of God.

Put those two ideas together, and we see that Jesus reveals God to us. He reveals the mind of God to us mere mortals. That was and continues to be a big part of His mission when He stepped out of His kingdom and stepped down into ours.

More specifically, Jesus is actively revealing God to you. Every time you open the pages of Scripture, you are encountering the mind of God. The Logos. The Christ. Every time you pull up a chair with Jesus at the table of your heart, you are soaking in that revelation and solidifying your connection to God.

Response

How does Jesus both complement and enhance the revelation of God through Scripture?

How does thinking of Jesus as the Logos—the "divine mind" or "divine reason"—help you better understand and experience at a personal level who He is and what He values?

SCRIPTURE MEMORY

If anyone acknowledges that Jesus is the Son of God, God lives in them and they in God.

—1 JOHN 4:15

DAY 4

Jesus Created Everything

For in him all things were created: things in heaven and on earth, visible and invisible, whether thrones or powers or rulers or authorities; all things have been created through him and for him.

COLOSSIANS 1:16

It's impossible to overstate the scope of our universe. That's because there's no way we can fully comprehend it. It's too vast for anyone to measure in any reliable way. But we can get a little taste of how huge the universe must be by thinking about the number of stars wheeling around us at any given moment.

Consider this: Our sun is so massive you could fit a million Earths inside it, yet our sun is just a tiny speck within our galaxy, the Milky Way, which contains about four hundred billion other stars. And the Milky Way is a tiny speck in the known universe. Astronomers estimate there are more than a hundred billion galaxies spinning and spiraling through the heavens. How many stars might there be in the universe? The official estimate is somewhere around 40^{22}, which in scientist language is 400 sextillion. If you wrote it out, you'd have a four followed by twenty-three zeros.[1]

Beyond sizes and spans, the incredible truth is that everything in the universe is connected, from the grandest galaxy all the way down to the smallest subatomic particle. That's because everything in the universe can be traced back to a single source: Jesus.

Scripture says it's through Jesus that "all things have been created." In other words, Jesus is the Creator of everything.

It's important to note that the phrase "all things" really does mean all things. Jesus is the Creator of all material things, which means everything that has mass, everything we can touch or measure or observe in some way. But Jesus is also the Creator of all nonmaterial things. He is the source of all love, for example. He is the source of all truth. He is the source of all goodness and mercy and grace.

Jesus is even the Creator of time. He's not bound by the minutes and months that cage all the experiences of our earthly lives. "All things have been created through him and for him."

Not only is Jesus the Creator of all things, but He also sustains all things. As we see in Colossians 1:17, "in him all things hold together." If you're watching TV and someone yanks the plug from the outlet, what happens? The screen goes blank. Whatever world or game or story you were immersed in suddenly disappears.

The same is true for what we know as reality. If Jesus were to somehow remove Himself from our world, everything that exists would no longer exist. Existence itself would cease to exist. The universe would wink and fade faster than a sparkler on the Fourth of July. Why? Because it would no longer be connected to its source of power. It would no longer be sustained by Christ.

Jesus is the Creator of everything. Jesus is the Sustainer of everything. And this same Jesus has made Himself available to you. This same Jesus is standing close, gesturing to you, *Why don't you pull up a chair?*

I hope you never lose sight of the wonder of that gift. The Author of life is interested in your life. The Creator of wisdom has offered you His wisdom. The power that fuels countless stars is available to sustain you and support you and guide you in every way.

Response

When has enjoying creation helped you feel especially connected to the Creator?

What obstacles sometimes prevent you from joining Jesus at your table?

SCRIPTURE MEMORY

If anyone acknowledges that Jesus is the Son of God, God lives in them and they in God.

—1 JOHN 4:15

DAY 5

Jesus Created You

Through him all things were made; without him nothing was made that has been made. In him was life, and that life was the light of all mankind.

JOHN 1:3-4

How big is a trillion? That number gets thrown around a lot these days, especially in connection with the economy and the national debt. And, yes, we just talked yesterday about there being trillions and trillions of stars in the universe. But the problem with using a word like *trillion* is that it's just a word. It's just a collection of letters. What does it actually mean?

Here's a way to visualize it. Let's say you were alive when Jesus was born, and you started to spend a million dollars every day from that point forward. If you somehow managed to live two thousand years to arrive at the present moment, you still wouldn't have spent a trillion dollars.

Here's another way. Let's say you counted to a million by saying one number every second. "One, two, three, four, five," and so on. If you were to stay at that pace—one number every second—it would take you eleven and a half days to hit one million. If you tried to count to a billion at that same pace, it would take you thirty-two years to finish. So obviously there's a huge difference between a million and a billion. What about a trillion, though? If you were to keep that same pace of one number every second, you would not reach a trillion until you had been counting for thirty-two thousand years![1]

I know you didn't pick up this book for a math lesson. But I wanted to illustrate just how big a trillion is because I want you to understand how crazy this next statement is: there are approximately thirty trillion cells in your body. Thirty trillion! Every single one of those cells carries out its function without you having to think about it. Every single one coordinates and cooperates with your system as a whole. And every single one includes your genetic code inside its DNA.

You are incredibly intricate, unimaginably complex, and exceedingly sophisticated. In a word, you are a miracle.

Specifically, you are a miracle created by Jesus. He designed you. He handcrafted every part of you and everything that makes you who you are. When Scripture says, "without him nothing was made that has been made," that includes you. And me. Everyone.

You have immeasurable value and worth.

No one reading these words is incidental or accidental. You were created on purpose and for a purpose.

Your life bears the signature of your master, almighty God. He knows everything about you—the good and the bad—yet He seeks to know you and invites you to know Him.

That is why He miraculously created you: to sit at the table with Him.

Response

What do you like best about yourself? Why?

What areas of your heart and mind are you trying to keep hidden from Christ?

SCRIPTURE MEMORY

If anyone acknowledges that Jesus is the Son of God, God lives in them and they in God.

—1 JOHN 4:15

DAY 6

Jesus Is Supreme

In the past God spoke to our ancestors through the prophets at many times and in various ways, but in these last days he has spoken to us by his Son, whom he appointed heir of all things, and through whom also he made the universe. The Son is the radiance of God's glory and the exact representation of his being, sustaining all things by his powerful word.
HEBREWS 1:1-3

There's no doubt we live in a world with lots of options. Tons of options. Probably too many options.

If you go to the grocery store, for example, you might think you're going to grab a bottle of ketchup real quick and go on your merry way. But then you actually reach the condiment aisle, and you realize there are at least thirty different versions of ketchup to choose from. Some are on sale. Some are organic. Some are brand names, and others are generic. Some are even called "catsup," whatever that is!

So you have options. But which option is best? Which bottle of ketchup will be the perfect choice to bring you maximum enjoyment at minimum cost? Having too many options can be a problem.

Unfortunately, many people approach their spiritual lives in a similar way. They look out over the world and see lots of religious systems in operation. Lots of gods. Lots of options. Even Christians can drift into that line of thinking: *Those religions might be good for some people, but Jesus is the best option for me.*

Please hear me: That's giving the Enemy a seat at your table. It's dangerous because Jesus is not the best choice among several worthy options—He is the *only* option. He is supreme.

That's what the author of Hebrews wanted to communicate. When you read that book, you quickly see a theme develop. The first two chapters make a point to show how Jesus is superior to angels in the spiritual realm. Chapter 3 shows how Jesus is superior to Moses—a bold statement when writing to the Jewish people. Chapters 4 through 7 show how Jesus is superior to the sacrificial system of the Old Testament, and chapter 8 circles back to show that Jesus' blood shed on the cross is superior to the blood of goats and rams. Chapters 9 and 10 speak of His sacrifice on the cross.

In fact, if you were to boil down all thirteen chapters in the book of Hebrews to just one phrase, it would probably be something like this: *Jesus is better.* The fancy doctrinal term for this is *the supremacy of Christ*, and it simply means Jesus is above everything else.

When you sit down at the table with Jesus, you are not sitting down with a good way to find salvation or even with the best way to develop a connection with God. Instead, Jesus is the only way. He is supreme. Because He is God.

Response

What would it look like for you to publicly proclaim that Jesus is supreme above all other gods and all other systems of religion?

What emotions would you experience if you made such a proclamation? Why?

SCRIPTURE MEMORY

If anyone acknowledges that Jesus is the Son of God, God lives in them and they in God.

—1 JOHN 4:15

Jesus Is Fully God and Fully Man

DAY 7

Jesus Is Human

But when the set time had fully come, God sent his Son, born of a woman, born under the law, to redeem those under the law, that we might receive adoption to sonship.
GALATIANS 4:4-5

Each childbirth is a unique moment, a singular event, in human history. Obviously, each person's birth is a powerful point in their own lives. None of us would be here without it! But the act itself is exceptional. It brings new life not only in an organic, physical sense, but also in the sense of a new moment of creation, a new genesis. Each baby born represents a new body, soul, and spirit. A new *person.*

What else can compare with that?

As you sit at the table with Jesus, remember that He experienced both Genesis and genesis. He spoke the universe into existence, and He also pulled the first gasps of air into tiny, previously unused lungs. Scripture says Jesus was "born of a woman," meaning He experienced both the miracle and the mess, just like you and I did. This was a real birth. There was a placenta. Somebody (probably Joseph) cut the umbilical cord that had connected Jesus to Mary for multiple months.

In other words, Jesus was born as a human being. A person. A man.

We saw in the previous section that Jesus is God. Fully God. He exists outside of time, and He is both the Creator and Sustainer of all things. It's strange, then, to say that Jesus is fully human. I want to acknowledge right off the bat that I understand how weird that is. Because I'm human, you're human, every person you've ever encountered is fully human. And none of us is divine. None of us looks or acts anything like God.

So, yeah, it's strange to say Jesus is God and human at the same time, but it's also true. And we know it's true because Scripture makes it crystal clear. John started his gospel by teaching that Jesus, the Word of God, "was God" and "was with God in the beginning" (1:1–2), meaning Jesus is God. Then, just twelve verses later, John said, "The Word became flesh and made his dwelling among us" (v. 14), meaning Jesus is human. He "became flesh."

The author of Hebrews wrote, "The Son is the radiance of God's glory and the exact representation of his being" (1:3), meaning Jesus is God. Then, just a chapter later, that same author wrote, "Since the children have flesh and blood, [Jesus] too shared in their humanity so that by his death he might break the power of him who holds the power of death—that is, the devil" (2:14), meaning Jesus is human. He shared in our humanity.

Just to be clear, it's important to know that Jesus isn't partly God and partly human. He isn't 90 percent God and 10 percent human or 50 percent God and 50 percent human. I know your calculator won't accept it, but Jesus is 100 percent God and 100 percent human. Completely one and completely the other. Fully both.

No, I don't understand how that's possible. Yes, I am grateful to share the table of my mind with Jesus who is both fully God and fully man.

Response

How would you define what it means to be human?

What are some similarities and differences between your human nature and Christ's?

SCRIPTURE MEMORY

The Word became flesh and made his dwelling among us. We have seen his glory, the glory of the one and only Son, who came from the Father, full of grace and truth.

—JOHN 1:14

DAY 8

Jesus Emptied Himself for Us

In your relationships with one another, have the same mindset as Christ Jesus:

Who, being in very nature God,
    did not consider equality with God something to be used
      to his own advantage;
rather, he made himself nothing
    by taking the very nature of a servant,
    being made in human likeness.

PHILIPPIANS 2:5-7

Hollywood has seen some major blockbusters hit movie theater screens across recent decades, and I think it's interesting to see how many of those really big, really successful films are rescue movies. *Star Wars* was a rescue movie: "Help me, Obi-Wan Kenobi, you're my only hope." *Saving Private Ryan* was a fantastic story about a group of soldiers making their way through occupied France in the middle of World War II and doing everything possible to rescue a needle out of a fully armed haystack. *Toy Story.* The Avengers movies.

One of the consistent themes you find in rescue movies is sacrifice. It's not enough for a hero simply to go find someone who's missing or in danger and then rescue them. Something needs to be lost in the process. Something needs to be voluntarily risked and then voluntarily released in order for true salvation to occur.

I think that's one of the reasons the gospel message resonates so deeply with people. Because when you understand Jesus is fully God, you really begin to understand what He gave up to take on flesh, join our world, and rescue us from our sin.

In Philippians 2, Paul wrote that Jesus "made himself nothing." The King James Version says Jesus "made himself of no reputation." The English Standard Version says he "emptied himself" by taking the form of a servant and being born in the likeness of men. This is another biblical truth that is difficult to understand, but it's important that we do understand it if we want to comprehend the full measure of what Christ has done for us.

Not only was Jesus fully human and fully God when He was born into our world, He was fully human and fully God when He walked the streets of Jerusalem, when He performed miracles, and even when He died. But that raises big questions. How could the fullness of God be stuffed into a human being? If you've ever tried to squeeze the last garbage bag into the trash can on trash day, you know how impossible that is. So how could an infinite God squeeze Himself into our little planet, let alone a human body? How could an all-powerful God be killed on a cross?

The answer is that Jesus emptied Himself. He made Himself nothing. He took on the form of a servant. Why? To rescue you and me. To save us. To bring us home.

Talk about a truth you can use to fortify your mind against the attacks of your enemies! Jesus stepped out of heaven to rescue you because you're worth rescuing. You're worth saving. You are precious to Him and always have been.

Response

Why were you in need of rescue before Jesus came into your life?

Who among your friends and family members needs to hear about Jesus' rescue mission?

SCRIPTURE MEMORY

The Word became flesh and made his dwelling among us. We have seen his glory, the glory of the one and only Son, who came from the Father, full of grace and truth.

—JOHN 1:14

DAY 9

Jesus Knew Temptation

Therefore, since we have a great high priest who has ascended into heaven, Jesus the Son of God, let us hold firmly to the faith we profess. For we do not have a high priest who is unable to empathize with our weaknesses, but we have one who has been tempted in every way, just as we are—yet he did not sin.
HEBREWS 4:14–15

Do you have a Captain Obvious in your life? I'm talking about someone who regularly verbalizes things that are obviously true. These are the people who sidle up next to you during a rainstorm and say, "Gonna be a wet one today." Or when you see them at a concert with their hands covering their ears, they can't help yelling out, "Wow, it's really loud in here!"

I say that because there's a Captain Obvious moment in the Bible that always makes me chuckle when I read it. At the beginning of Matthew 4, the text says Jesus was led by the Spirit into the wilderness to be tempted by the Devil. Then comes verse 2: "After fasting forty days and forty nights, he was hungry."

There it is! Jesus spent forty days and forty nights in the wilderness without a bite of food. Not even a crumb. That's like going the whole month of January without eating because you made a New Year's resolution. Oh, and also the first week of February. And then waiting three more days before you finally snagged a bowl of soup on February 10.

Of course Jesus was hungry! I'm pretty sure I would've been dead.

Don't get me wrong, I'm not knocking Scripture here. I don't think Matthew was giving us unnecessary information. Actually, I think this verse is very helpful. Why? Because it reminds us that Jesus is human not just in some abstract way but in real life.

When Jesus didn't eat, He got hungry. When He was in the shop with Joseph, learning to be a carpenter, there were times He banged His thumb with a hammer—assuming they had hammers in those days—and it hurt. He bled from cuts. He slipped on gravel while walking up and down the hills of Nazareth. He had favorite meals, and He probably thought some vegetables didn't taste that great. (Maybe.)

Not only that, but Scripture says Jesus "has been tempted in every way, just as we are." Think about that for a moment. Think of those areas of temptation that cause you trouble: gluttony, anger, lust, laziness, sneakiness, deception, and so on. *Jesus knows what that's like!* He's felt the same types of temptation. Yes, the text makes it clear "he did not sin," but the point is, Christ has been in your shoes. He knows what it means to have a clear understanding of God's will and to feel pulled in another direction.

That's great news for you, because when you sit down at the table with Jesus, you're not spending time with some prude who looks at you with disapproval whenever you make a mistake: *tsk, tsk, tsk.* No, you're giving access to a friend who can empathize with your weaknesses and help you make better choices. You're giving influence to a Savior who offers mercy and grace during your time of need.

Response

Where do you need mercy and grace in your life right now?

What are practical ways you can turn to Jesus during moments of temptation?

SCRIPTURE MEMORY

The Word became flesh and made his dwelling among us. We have seen his glory, the glory of the one and only Son, who came from the Father, full of grace and truth.

—JOHN 1:14

DAY 10

Jesus Is a Historical Person

Very early in the morning, the chief priests, with the elders, the teachers of the law and the whole Sanhedrin, made their plans. So they bound Jesus, led him away and handed him over to Pilate.

"Are you the king of the Jews?" asked Pilate.

"You have said so," Jesus replied.

MARK 15:1–2

When we look back at the history of the world, and especially the history of specific countries, it's easy to identify those people who were so important, so influential in their day and beyond, that they take on an almost mythical quality. George Washington and Susan B. Anthony are good examples from the United States. Queen Elizabeth II and Winston Churchill qualify for England. Nelson Mandela from South Africa. Mohandas Gandhi from India.

These are individuals who seem larger than life. They've been memorialized in paintings and sculptures. Their names are on schools and streets throughout the world. Their legends carry so much weight that it's easy to forget they started out as regular people.

If we're not careful, we can push this tendency to an extreme when it comes to Jesus. We can start to think of Him as a legend or a character from a story rather than acknowledge Him as a historical person.

And make no mistake: Jesus is a historical person. He was born in a village called Bethlehem and grew up in another town called Nazareth. Both places exist today. You can visit them. You can see the place on the edge of Nazareth where Jesus' neighbors tried to kill Him by throwing Him off a cliff (Luke 4:29). Jesus sailed on the Sea of Galilee and ate fish from those waters. He walked the streets of Jerusalem and taught on the steps of the temple, some of which are still standing today.

People who think Jesus wasn't a real person often say the only evidence for His existence is in the Bible. That's not the case. There's loads of historical evidence for Jesus' life, death, and resurrection just sitting out there for anyone willing to look and see, to read and learn.

For example, the Jewish historian Josephus mentioned Jesus several times in his writings, including a mention of James, "the brother of Jesus-who-is-called-Messiah." James was a common name in that day. So was Jesus. So Josephus gave some extra detail to clarify which Jesus he was talking about: the one called the Messiah.

Tacitus is another example, and he was maybe the most famous Roman historian of that time. Writing in a book titled *Annals*, Tacitus described Christians in this way: "The founder of this name, Christ [*Christus* in Latin], had been executed in the reign of Tiberius by the procurator Pontius Pilate. . . . Suppressed for a time, the deadly superstition erupted again not only in Judea, the origin of this evil, but also in the city [Rome], where all things horrible and shameful from everywhere come together and become popular."[1]

Obviously, Tacitus wasn't a fan of Christians. But that didn't stop him from confirming Jesus' life, His death, and the aftershocks of His resurrection. That didn't stop him from confirming the historical detail of Pontius Pilate presiding over Jesus' crucifixion.

Why? Because Jesus is a historical person. And His impact on human history is unmatched.

When you sit down at the table with Jesus, then, you're not sitting down with a character. You're not being fortified by a figment of your imagination. No, you're deepening your connection with the One who walked on water. With the Teacher who still teaches. With the Healer who still heals.

Response

Why is it important to recognize and defend the truth that Jesus was present in human history?

What are some of the ways Jesus has impacted human history?

SCRIPTURE MEMORY

The Word became flesh and made his dwelling among us. We have seen his glory, the glory of the one and only Son, who came from the Father, full of grace and truth.

—JOHN 1:14

DAY 11

Jesus Is the Son of Man

Jesus said to them, "Truly I tell you, at the renewal of all things, when the Son of Man sits on his glorious throne, you who have followed me will also sit on twelve thrones, judging the twelve tribes of Israel."
MATTHEW 19:28

Have you noticed how many titles are floating out there in our society? There are everyday titles, of course, such as *Mr., Mrs., Ms., madam, sir,* and so on. Those are common. Professionally, you've got occupational titles like *doctor, officer, captain, senator,* and *judge.* When it comes to actual job titles within an organization, you have to wade through the alphabet soup of *CEO, CFO, COO, CIO,* and *CMO,* not to mention *president, vice president, chairman of the board,* and so on.

Jesus carried several titles during His public ministry. Demons and others who understood His true nature regularly referred to Him as the "Son of God." Of course, *Christ* and *Messiah* are titles commonly connected with Jesus today, although He typically avoided those modifiers during His ministry because He knew that publicly claiming to be the Messiah—the Christ—would get Him arrested and eventually killed. So He was biding His time.

There's one title Jesus used for Himself—*Son of Man.* In fact, He used it often when referring to Himself: "When the Son of Man sits on his glorious throne, you who have followed me will also sit on twelve thrones."

Son of Man is an interesting title because it can be interpreted in two ways. First, it was often used in Jesus' day and before to mark a person of distinction, someone who was worthy of interest but at their core was just a human being. For example, God referred to the prophet Ezekiel as "son of man" more than ninety times.

So, in that sense, to be a son of man was simply to be human.

But the second interpretation of Son of Man was much different. Hundreds of years before Jesus' birth, the prophet Daniel received a vision of the future Messiah, the future Savior who would rescue God's people. Here's what he saw:

> In my vision at night I looked, and there before me was one like a son of man, coming with the clouds of heaven. He approached the Ancient of Days and was led into his presence. He was given authority, glory and sovereign power; all nations and peoples of every language worshiped him. His dominion is an everlasting dominion that will not pass away, and his kingdom is one that will never be destroyed. (Dan. 7:13–14)

With the benefit of history, we understand this entire vision was pointing forward to Jesus. He is the One given authority, glory, and power. He is the rightful King and Ruler over all peoples and all nations, and His kingdom will never be destroyed.

Take a moment to let that sink in. Jesus is the subject of ancient prophecies from thousands of years ago, and Jesus is seated right there next to you. His authority opens doors for you. His glory illuminates you. And His power protects your mind and your heart against the attacks of those who wish you harm.

Response

What are some specific ways you have benefited from Jesus' humanity?

What are some specific ways you have benefited from Jesus' role as the Messiah? The Savior?

SCRIPTURE MEMORY

The Word became flesh and made his dwelling among us. We have seen his glory, the glory of the one and only Son, who came from the Father, full of grace and truth.

—JOHN 1:14

Jesus Is God with Us

But after he had considered this, an angel of the Lord appeared to him in a dream and said, "Joseph son of David, do not be afraid to take Mary home as your wife, because what is conceived in her is from the Holy Spirit. She will give birth to a son, and you are to give him the name Jesus, because he will save his people from their sins."

All this took place to fulfill what the Lord had said through the prophet: "The virgin will conceive and give birth to a son, and they will call him Immanuel" (which means "God with us").

MATTHEW 1:20-23

Without a doubt, Christmas is one of the best seasons of the year. Yes, I know it's hectic. Yes, I know it can be expensive. Yes, I know gathering with family is not always as fun as it should be. And, yes, I know there is usually at least one moment when you're ready to throw your hands in the air and escape to an isolated cabin or a deserted island. Me too.

But when you push all that aside and get right down to the core of things, Christmas is about God coming near. It's about God stepping inside. As the prophet Isaiah said so many thousands of years ago, Christmas is about "God with us"—which means Christmas is all about Jesus.

Jesus is Immanuel, meaning "God with us." What's important, though, is that the incarnation of Christ was not the first time God stepped in close to be with humanity. No, God has been with us from the beginning.

Genesis 3 reminds us that God was in the habit of walking with Adam and Eve in the garden of Eden. He often joined them "in the cool of the day" (v. 8). Just to hang out. Just to be with them and enjoy their company. That's God with us.

Speaking with Abraham, God promised, "I will establish my covenant as an everlasting covenant between me and you and your descendants after you for the generations to come, to be your God and the God of your descendants after you" (17:7). Yes, this moment is often framed around God's covenant with Abraham—a legal agreement. But don't miss the personal element there. The Creator of the universe knelt down to Abraham and said, "I will be *your God.*" That's God with us.

Exodus records this incredible statement: "The LORD would speak to Moses face to face, as one speaks to a friend" (33:11). When Solomon brought the ark of the covenant into God's house, God's presence so saturated the temple that "the priests could not perform their service because of the cloud, for the glory of the LORD filled his temple" (1 Kings 8:11). And all throughout the Old Testament, God's promise resounded over and over to humanity: "You will be my people, and I will be your God" (Jer. 30:22). That's God with us.

Throughout history, every time humanity has tried to push God away through rebellion or sin, He has responded by taking another step closer, another step nearer, another step deeper into the mess of our world. That is exactly how Jesus arrived. He is the ultimate fulfillment of God's promise to be with us.

And that is why I hope you will join Him at the table even at this moment. He is not just God with us; He is God with you. Whenever you mess up, He moves in a little closer. Whenever you fail, He feels your shame and reaches out to set things right, to fortify your mind.

Response

When have you felt a special closeness to Jesus?

What steps can you take today to actively and intentionally seek His presence?

SCRIPTURE MEMORY

The Word became flesh and made his dwelling among us. We have seen his glory, the glory of the one and only Son, who came from the Father, full of grace and truth.

—JOHN 1:14

Jesus Is Our Glorious Savior

DAY 13

Jesus Is Savior

They said to the woman, "We no longer believe just because of what you said; now we have heard for ourselves, and we know that this man really is the Savior of the world."
JOHN 4:42

Have you noticed that saviors are out of fashion these days? We used to have a pretty cut-and-dried formula when it came to building a hero. Start with a good backstory, throw in some bulging biceps and chiseled abs, then finish with a splash of unquestioned virtue. Maybe add a clever catchphrase for marketing purposes. In modern movies, Captain America and Wonder Woman are the only heroes I can think of that still follow that formula.

In today's culture, we mostly prefer antiheroes over saviors. We like protagonists who look and talk a little more like antagonists. When they run (or fly) into action, they carry some baggage with them. They make mistakes. They blur the lines between good and bad, right and wrong, functional and inspirational.

Maybe that's why so many people have trouble believing the reality of who Jesus is and everything He accomplished, because Jesus is nothing like Walter White (*Breaking Bad*) or the Merc with a Mouth (*Deadpool*). Jesus is a Savior to the core.

I love the way Jesus' character shines through in His encounter with the Samaritan woman. If you've heard that story before, you might remember that the Samaritans and Jews were mortal enemies. Think of the ethnic conflicts raging today—Israelis and Palestinians,

Sunnis and Shias. That's how much the Jews disliked the Samaritans. And the feeling was pretty much mutual.

Yet, while Jesus and His disciples were traveling, He decided to make a pit stop in a town called Sychar in Samaria. And when a woman from that town approached the well where Jesus was sitting, He did not ignore her, as was the custom of the day. Instead, He initiated a conversation. Why? Because there at the well, Jesus understood this woman was drowning—not in water, but in sin. She was drowning in the consequences of poor options and poor choices.

Jesus reached out to save this woman not because it was convenient for Him, and not because He wanted to expand His brand into the Samaritan community. No, He reached out simply because He is a Savior. He is *the* Savior. Reaching out to those in need is central to His nature and character. In fact, reaching out to those in need was (and is) the centerpiece of His mission and purpose. It's what He lives for.

Not only did Jesus reach out to this woman with the offer of salvation, but He also extended that offer to the entire town. Remember, these people would have hated Him on sight because He was Jewish, yet it took Jesus only two days to completely turn that hatred into wonder. "We no longer believe just because of what you said," the townspeople told the Samaritan woman. "Now we have heard for ourselves, and we know that this man really is the Savior of the world."

Have you heard for yourself? Do you know that Jesus saves? Have you made the same decision as those townspeople all those centuries ago? If so, do your actions reflect that choice each day? If not, He is reaching out for you even now. So pull up a chair. Sit close. Let the Savior start a conversation and see where He takes you.

Response

How would you describe or summarize Jesus' role as Savior?

Where will you have opportunities this week to introduce Jesus to others who need saving?

SCRIPTURE MEMORY

Salvation is found in no one else, for there is no other name under heaven given to mankind by which we must be saved.

—ACTS 4:12

DAY 14

Jesus Is the Christ

The woman said, "I know that Messiah" (called Christ) "is coming. When he comes, he will explain everything to us."
Then Jesus declared, "I, the one speaking to you—I am he."
JOHN 4:25-26

Is there anything more satisfying than a dream fulfilled? A promise kept? Is there anything more wonderful than waiting for something you deeply desire, waiting for it so long that you almost, *almost* give up, and then watching that desire come true?

I can't think of anything better.

The people of Jesus' day carried just such a desire, and they carried it deep within their hearts. That desire was based on a promise God had made many times throughout the Scriptures—what we know as the Old Testament. Specifically, God had promised that someone would come to make the world right once more. Someone would come to fix what had been broken and restore what had been lost. In other words, someone would come as Savior.

For the descendants of Abraham and Isaac, both Jew and Samaritan, that promise could be summarized in one word: *Messiah*. Or, in the Greek language, *Christ*. (Those terms are interchangeable.)

God's promise began in Genesis 3, right after Adam and Eve's rebellious choice brought sin into the world. Speaking to the serpent, God told of a descendant of Eve who would eventually defeat Satan once and for all: "He will crush your head, and you will strike his heel" (v. 15).

45

God reaffirmed that promise to Abraham when He said, "I will bless those who bless you, and whoever curses you I will curse; and all peoples on earth will be blessed through you" (12:3). Not only would Messiah crush Satan, but He would bless "all peoples on earth." His power and goodness would spread beyond the Jewish people and extend to the whole world.

Moses spoke of this promise when he said, "The LORD your God will raise up for you a prophet like me from among you, from your fellow Israelites. You must listen to him" (Deut. 18:15). When God told David, "Your house and your kingdom will endure forever before me; your throne will be established forever" (2 Sam. 7:16), He made it clear that Messiah would come from David's line. And Daniel saw a vision of God's promise fulfilled when he described "one like a son of man, coming with the clouds of heaven," one who "was given authority, glory and sovereign power" and whose "kingdom is one that will never be destroyed" (Dan. 7:13–14).

For centuries, God's people had waited for that promise to come true. They had waited for Messiah to enter the world and accomplish His extraordinary work. Can you imagine, then, what it must have been like for that Samaritan woman—that regular, unheralded, underappreciated woman at the well—to sit in front of Jesus and hear Him say, "I, the one speaking to you—I am he"?

To her credit, she knew the truth right away. She believed.

What about you? Don't let anyone tell you you're not important enough. Don't let any enemy hiss their lies about who you are—the wrong color, the wrong age, the wrong neighborhood, the wrong whatever. Jesus is Messiah, and He says you matter. He is the Christ, and He set a place at the table of your mind as the fulfillment of the greatest promise ever made.

Response

What promises are you waiting for God to fulfill?

In what ways has Jesus fulfilled the role of Messiah, the Savior who makes all things right? In what ways is that fulfillment still to come?

SCRIPTURE MEMORY

Salvation is found in no one else, for there is no other name under heaven given to mankind by which we must be saved.

—ACTS 4:12

DAY 15

Jesus Saves Us from Sin

[Jesus] went on: "What comes out of a person is what defiles them. For it is from within, out of a person's heart, that evil thoughts come—sexual immorality, theft, murder, adultery, greed, malice, deceit, lewdness, envy, slander, arrogance and folly. All these evils come from inside and defile a person."

MARK 7:20–23

Salvation is a big topic for the church. A big buzz word. But what about us personally? What does that word mean for you and me and those we care about?

We've spent a couple of days already exploring that Jesus is Messiah, the Christ; He is the Savior of the world sent to rescue people like you and me. But that raises a big question: Save us from what? Rescue us from what? What is the problem Jesus came to solve on our behalf?

The big answer is sin.

I know—that's not a popular word. Those three little letters feel too churchy. Too judgmental. Too uncomfortable. But the reality is we'll never have a proper understanding of Jesus until we come to grips with sin. More to the point, we'll never have a proper understanding of Jesus until we come to grips with *our own* sin. Mine. Yours.

What is sin? There are lots of definitions out there. Missing the mark of God's standard. Disobedience to God's will. Rebellion against God. All of those definitions are true, and all of them boil down to pretty much the same thing on a practical level. As James wrote, "If anyone, then, knows the good they ought to do and doesn't do it, it is sin for them" (4:17).

The problem is sin doesn't exist out there in the ether. It's not floating around like a malignant virus trying to latch on and push us in the wrong direction. As Jesus said, our sin is "from within, out of a person's heart." That's why we constantly struggle with immorality, greed, anger, deception, envy, malice, and so much more. The sinful things we do are based not on wrong choices we make in our minds but on *who we are at the core*. We are corrupted from the inside out.

What's even worse news is that sin doesn't make us bad; it makes us spiritually dead (Rom. 6:23). A bad person can try to improve themselves, but a dead person cannot do one thing to improve their situation, their state.

And that's why we need to be rescued. We could no more solve the problem of our own sinfulness than a man suffering from cardiac disease can heal himself by ripping out his own heart. We need the spiritual equivalent of a heart transplant. We need to be transformed from the inside out.

In other words, we need salvation. We need the healing work of Jesus, the Christ, who is our Savior.

Here's why the gospel is often called the good news: Not only do we need it, but we already have it. I have it. I feel it. I'm not the same person I used to be. I've been changed from the inside out, and I'm still being changed each and every day. I'm saved from my sin.

If you've experienced salvation, then you have that healing, that transformation, also. You're not the same person you used to be. You're new. And if you've never been there, if you've never felt that, you can. Right now, right this moment. You just need to meet your Savior.

Response

Where do you see evidence of sin in the world today?

Where do you see evidence of sin in your own life, and how is Jesus rescuing you from its stranglehold?

SCRIPTURE MEMORY

Salvation is found in no one else, for there is no other name under heaven given to mankind by which we must be saved.

—ACTS 4:12

Jesus Saves Us from Evil

> But when the Pharisees heard this, they said, "It is only by Beelzebul, the prince of demons, that this fellow drives out demons."
>
> Jesus knew their thoughts and said to them, "Every kingdom divided against itself will be ruined, and every city or household divided against itself will not stand. If Satan drives out Satan, he is divided against himself. How then can his kingdom stand? . . . But if it is by the Spirit of God that I drive out demons, then the kingdom of God has come upon you."
>
> MATTHEW 12:24-26, 28

The Declaration of Independence was signed in 1776, which means the United States of America has existed as a nation for 245 years at the time of this writing. We have 245 years of history as a country. Now, can you guess how many of those 245 years the USA has been at war?

The answer is 228. Does that surprise you? It sure surprised me! That includes the big wars, such as the Revolutionary War, the Civil War, World Wars I and II, Vietnam, Iraq, Afghanistan, and so on. But it also includes conflicts with Native Americans, conflicts with Mexico, rebellions, the Cold War with Russia, and more. In the entire history of our nation, we have experienced only 17 years of peace.[1]

Here's a truth that might surprise you even more: if you're a member of God's kingdom, you've been at war your entire life. In fact, you are at war right this second. I'm not talking about a physical war with bombs and guns, but I am talking about a real conflict, a real battle.

Specifically, you are in a spiritual battle against evil.

In Matthew 12, Jesus had to remind the Pharisees and other religious leaders about this war, this conflict. The Pharisees couldn't deny that Jesus cast out demons and demonstrated authority over the forces of evil, but they did come up with an excuse. They declared Jesus could fight against evil only because He was evil Himself!

Of course, everyone understood that was stupid. Still, it gave Jesus a chance to remind everyone of the stakes in the battle against evil. According to Jesus, there are two kingdoms that exist in our world and every other: God's kingdom and the kingdom of Satan (whom the Pharisees called Beelzebul). These kingdoms have been at war ever since Satan rebelled against God and was cast out of heaven.

The bad news for us is that evil really does exist. Evil forces really do exist, including demons. Paul made that clear in Ephesians: "For our struggle is not against flesh and blood, but against the rulers, against the authorities, against the powers of this dark world and against the spiritual forces of evil in the heavenly realms" (6:12). These evil forces impact our world. They are active in attacking members of God's kingdom, and their attacks can produce temptation, suffering, grief, and pain.

The good news for us is that Satan's kingdom is already defeated. Christ our Savior won the victory against evil when He died on the cross to pay the penalty for sin and then rose from the grave in glory. But this means you are certainly in the middle of this spiritual battle—as you always will be on this side of eternity—yet the war has already been won.

Response

What have you been taught about demons and other evil forces?

What are active, practical ways we can participate in the spiritual battle around us?

SCRIPTURE MEMORY

Salvation is found in no one else, for there is no other name under heaven given to mankind by which we must be saved.

—ACTS 4:12

Jesus Saves Us from Death

For God so loved the world that he gave his one and only Son, that whoever believes in him shall not perish but have eternal life. For God did not send his Son into the world to condemn the world, but to save the world through him.
JOHN 3:16-17

Way back in the 1600s, the poet John Donne wrote a challenge to death, a call to arms. Here's how it starts:

> Death, be not proud, though some have called thee
> Mighty and dreadful, for thou art not so;
> For those whom thou think'st thou dost overthrow
> Die not, poor Death, nor yet canst thou kill me.[1]

I love the image of a man standing up in front of the grim reaper, arms raised and chin high. "You think you're mighty, Death? You think you're dreadful? Come at me, bro!"

The irony is that Donne's poem was published in 1633, but Donne himself actually died in 1631. His challenge to death was published posthumously. Does that mean John Donne was a fool? A fraud? A naive wannabe? Nope. It just means he understood his place in God's kingdom. Donne had been sitting at the table with Jesus for a long time, and he was ready for the next step.

We've seen in recent days that Jesus Christ is the Savior of the world. He saves us from sin. He saves us from the forces of evil and their efforts to destroy us. And ultimately He saves us from death. Not physical death, of course, not the death of the external shell we call our bodies. Instead, Jesus saves us from what many scholars call spiritual death—eternal death.

That's the promise of John 3:16, which some consider to be the most famous verse in the Bible: "Whoever believes in him shall not perish but have eternal life." Because Jesus rose from the dead, because He defeated death and saved us from the consequences of our sin, you and I can experience eternal life. We can live forever in God's kingdom and enjoy an eternal relationship with Him rather than be separated from Him.

Now, there's a common misconception about eternal life that is worth correcting. Namely, a lot of people (including a lot of Christians) think eternal life starts when our physical bodies die. That's not the case.

Look at what Jesus said later in John 3: "Whoever believes in the Son has eternal life" (v. 36). Notice the present tense there: "has," not "will have." Later, Jesus was praying to the Father and said, "Now this is eternal life: that they know you, the only true God, and Jesus Christ, whom you have sent" (17:3). Eternal life begins the moment you are born again into a relationship with Jesus.

Basically, if you know Jesus, if you have experienced His salvation and are living as His disciple, then eternal life has already started. It's here. It's now. It will be even better when you shed your body, step into heaven, and see your Savior face to face.

Response

How does the reality of death influence your life?

How should understanding that we are currently experiencing eternal life affect us today?

SCRIPTURE MEMORY

Salvation is found in no one else, for there is no other name under heaven given to mankind by which we must be saved.

—ACTS 4:12

DAY 18

Jesus Is Your Savior

I urge, then, first of all, that petitions, prayers, intercession and thanksgiving be made for all people—for kings and all those in authority, that we may live peaceful and quiet lives in all godliness and holiness. This is good, and pleases God our Savior, who wants all people to be saved and to come to a knowledge of the truth.
1 TIMOTHY 2:1–4

I'll be the first to admit there are a lot of clichés that get overused in the church. "Whenever God closes a door, He always opens a window." "God will never give you more than you can handle." "You know He works in mysterious ways." I don't know if I've ever heard one of these phrases in a situation where it was actually helpful.

Here's another one I've encountered several times: "If you were the only person alive on planet Earth, Jesus would still have died on the cross to save you from your sins." If you're like me, that idea comes across as a little impractical. A little strange. A little too hypothetical.

But it's also 100 percent true.

As Paul wrote to his spiritual son Timothy, "God our Savior"—that's Jesus—"wants all people to be saved and to come to a knowledge of the truth." Jesus actively desires for all people to be saved. That means every single person who has ever lived, who is living now, and who will live at any point in the future.

Yes, Scripture describes Jesus as the Savior of the world, but Jesus did not embark on His divine rescue mission to save humanity in general; He came to save individual humans. He came to save people with specific names and personalities and fingerprints. People like you and me.

Remember, Jesus is the Creator of everything and everyone. Jesus knows the distinctive character sequence of your DNA. He handcrafted you from the moment of conception until right now. As the psalmist proclaimed to God, "For you created my inmost being; you knit me together in my mother's womb. I praise you because I am fearfully and wonderfully made" (Ps. 139:13–14).

Not only that, but Scripture says God "chose us in him before the creation of the world to be holy and blameless in his sight. In love he predestined us for adoption to sonship through Jesus Christ, in accordance with his pleasure and will" (Eph. 1:4–5). This means that before Jesus spoke one atom into existence in our universe, you were on His mind.

Best of all, you are on His mind still. You are on His mind right now, right this second. So you have an opportunity right now, right this second, to sit down at the table with your Savior. Don't miss that: to sit with *your* Savior and allow Him to fortify your mind, to strengthen you and bless you, and to continue His good work in your life.

Response

What emotions did you experience while reading the content above?

How can you take advantage of the truth that Jesus knows you and cares for you personally?

SCRIPTURE MEMORY

Salvation is found in no one else, for there is no other name under heaven given to mankind by which we must be saved.

—ACTS 4:12

Jesus Is Our Teacher

DAY 19

Jesus Is Rabbi

Turning around, Jesus saw them following and asked, "What do you want?"

They said, "Rabbi" (which means "Teacher"), "where are you staying?"

"Come," he replied, "and you will see."

JOHN 1:38-39

If I were to ask you what Jesus' occupation was, you would probably say He was a carpenter. And you'd be right—for the most part. Joseph was a carpenter, and it seems clear from Scripture that he took on Jesus as an apprentice in that field. When Jesus returned to His hometown at the beginning of His public ministry, the people asked, "Isn't this the carpenter? Isn't this Mary's son and the brother of James, Joseph, Judas and Simon? Aren't his sisters here with us?" (Mark 6:3).

So, yes, Jesus was a carpenter. Later in life, though, He intentionally shifted away from that business to become a teacher. More specifically, a rabbi.

The Jewish culture of the ancient world placed a high value on education, although that privilege was typically limited to sons. When a boy approached the age of thirteen, he would usually leave school and enter the real world by becoming an apprentice in a trade: farmer, fisherman, blacksmith, tentmaker, carpenter, and so on.

That wasn't the case for the very best students, however. They continued their education. After several more years of study, the most successful students would hope to be chosen by an established rabbi to serve as one of his disciples. And after several more years of serving and learning from that rabbi, the most successful disciples would become rabbis themselves. This usually happened around age thirty.

What does Scripture say? "Now Jesus himself was about thirty years old when he began his ministry" (Luke 3:23). Right in line with becoming a rabbi. Jesus left Nazareth and began traveling throughout Galilee and other regions, teaching about the kingdom of God—a common practice for the rabbis of His day. And as Jesus traveled, He also gathered a group of disciples who joined Him, learned from Him, helped in His ministry, and committed themselves to living alongside him.

In short, Jesus intentionally lived and functioned as a rabbi—a teacher.

Interestingly, Jesus didn't choose His disciples from the academic cream of the crop. Instead, He chose fishermen. A tax collector. Even a zealot (what we might call a freedom fighter). He chose regular people to teach, lead, and mentor—people like you and me.

And that's the wonderful opportunity you and I still have today. We can follow Rabbi Jesus. We can learn from our Teacher. We can live as His disciples, joining Him in ministry, helping to advance His kingdom, and committing ourselves to living just as He lives.

Over the next few days we're going to explore portions from two of Jesus' most famous sermons, known to many as the Sermon on the Mount and the Olivet Discourse. What better way to fortify our minds?

Response

Who are some teachers who influenced your life in positive ways?

How did Jesus' role as a rabbi help fulfill His mission to save humanity from our sins?

SCRIPTURE MEMORY

The student is not above the teacher, but everyone who is fully trained will be like their teacher.

—LUKE 6:40

DAY 20

Jesus Taught Us to Raise the Stakes

If you love those who love you, what reward will you get? Are not even the tax collectors doing that? And if you greet only your own people, what are you doing more than others? Do not even pagans do that? Be perfect, therefore, as your heavenly Father is perfect.

MATTHEW 5:46–48

There's been a lot of conversation in recent years about participation trophies, the practice of giving awards to kids not because they won something—a sporting event or an academic competition—but simply because they engaged in the activity.

I'm not qualified to jump in with an opinion on whether giving kids those trophies is good or bad. But I sure do think far too many people are awarding themselves participation trophies in their spiritual lives. There are way too many Christians who pat themselves on the back for wearing a Jesus jersey while sitting on the spiritual sidelines; way too many Christians who settle for good enough rather than striving for excellence.

In the Sermon on the Mount, Jesus had something to say to such Christians. Actually, He had a lot to say, and He kept using the same phrase over and over again to say it. See if you can pick up the pattern in what He taught:

- "You have heard that it was said to the people long ago, 'You shall not murder, and anyone who murders will be subject to judgment.' But I tell you that anyone who is angry with a brother or sister will be subject to judgment" (Matt. 5:21–22).

- "You have heard that it was said, 'You shall not commit adultery.' But I tell you that anyone who looks at a woman lustfully has already committed adultery with her in his heart" (vv. 27–28).

- "It has been said, 'Anyone who divorces his wife must give her a certificate of divorce.' But I tell you that anyone who divorces his wife, except for sexual immorality, makes her the victim of adultery, and anyone who marries a divorced woman commits adultery" (vv. 31–32).

- "You have heard that it was said, 'Eye for eye, and tooth for tooth.' But I tell you, do not resist an evil person. If anyone slaps you on the right cheek, turn to them the other cheek also" (vv. 38–39).

Do you see the pattern? "You have heard . . . But I tell you . . ." One thing Jesus wanted to do here was remind us who is worth listening to and who is not. What Jesus has to say will always be far better and far more helpful than what the world is shouting in our ears.

But that's not all Jesus was trying to teach us. He was also raising the stakes in our spiritual lives.

As Christians, we've all heard what it takes to do the minimum. We all understand what it takes to get by on a spiritual level, to be good enough, to settle. *Don't do the really bad stuff. Do all the things you're expected to do and say all the things you're supposed to say. Don't get in trouble.*

But Jesus taught us to look higher, to strive for spiritual excellence. In His words, to "be perfect . . . as your heavenly Father is perfect." The goal is to be like Jesus. That's what He taught in His most famous sermon, and that's what He'll teach you when you join Him at the table.

Response

What are some of the things all Christians are expected to do? To avoid?

Who is an example of spiritual excellence that you would like to follow?

SCRIPTURE MEMORY

The student is not above the teacher, but everyone who is fully trained will be like their teacher.

—LUKE 6:40

DAY 21

Jesus Taught Us
How to Pray

**But when you pray, go into your room, close the door and
pray to your Father, who is unseen. Then your Father, who
sees what is done in secret, will reward you.**
MATTHEW 6:6

The Guinness world record for the longest conversation (telephone or
video) is fifty-four hours and four minutes. The record is shared by
four people, all residents of Latvia: Kristaps Štāls, Patriks Zvaigzne,
Leonids Romanovs, and Tatjana Fjodorova. The two pairs of talkers
set the record in a shopping mall as part of a sponsored event in
2012.[1]

Talk about a wandering conversation!

Speaking of conversations, that's what prayer is supposed to be: a
conversation between us and God. Not *us* in a general or a corporate
sense, of course, but *us* as in you and me, as individuals. That's one of
the truths Jesus communicated in His Sermon on the Mount.

When you read through Matthew 6, you see several instances
where Jesus taught His hearers that our spiritual lives should never
be treated as a show. "Be careful not to practice your righteousness in
front of others to be seen by them," He said. "If you do, you will have
no reward from your Father in heaven" (v. 1).

Specifically, Jesus taught His followers to avoid making a show of
their giving. "So when you give to the needy, do not announce it with

trumpets, as the hypocrites do in the synagogues and on the streets, to be honored by others" (v. 2). The temple at Jerusalem had a large collection drum near the entrance that functioned as the equivalent of an offering plate. People would walk by those drums and add their money to the collection. Of course, since all money back then was metal coins, giving to the Lord could produce quite a racket. Some people really enjoyed dumping in a pile of coins as loudly and ostentatiously as they could so that others would see and hear them.

Later in the chapter, Jesus said, "When you fast, do not look somber as the hypocrites do, for they disfigure their faces to show others they are fasting. Truly I tell you, they have received their reward in full" (v. 16). This is the same principle at work. There were many people of Jesus' day who liked to make a show of their fasting. *Look how hungry I am! Look how spiritual I am!*

The same principle applied to prayer. "And when you pray," Jesus taught, "do not be like the hypocrites, for they love to pray standing in the synagogues and on the street corners to be seen by others" (v. 5). Instead, He instructed His followers to be different: "But when you pray, go into your room, close the door and pray to your Father, who is unseen. Then your Father, who sees what is done in secret, will reward you."

Jesus wanted His followers to understand that prayer is not a show. It's not something we do to be seen as impressive or inspiring or pious—or even to be seen at all. Instead, prayer is a private conversation with our heavenly Father, who loves us. A conversation that should continue not just for fifty-four hours and four minutes but throughout our entire lives.

Response

Who taught you how to pray?

What are your biggest struggles with prayer?

SCRIPTURE MEMORY

The student is not above the teacher, but everyone who is fully trained will be like their teacher.

—LUKE 6:40

Jesus Taught About False Teachers

Watch out for false prophets. They come to you in sheep's clothing, but inwardly they are ferocious wolves.

MATTHEW 7:15

Because I travel often, I have a pretty close relationship with the GPS app on my phone. It helps get me where I need to go even when I don't know where I'm going. Sometimes I don't know what I would do without it.

Still, GPS isn't perfect, as one long-haul driver discovered outside Silverton, Colorado. The driver was operating a thirty-foot box truck and following GPS directions to his intended destination several towns away. However, those directions instructed him to drive through an area locals called Engineer Pass, a rugged mountain road with an elevation of almost thirteen thousand feet. Successfully navigating that pass typically requires a four-wheel-drive vehicle—and a lot of luck. Unsurprisingly, the truck became stuck and blocked traffic on that road for days.[1]

Nobody likes to be led astray. When receiving bad directions from our GPS, we typically experience some minor inconvenience at the worst. When we get bad directions in our spiritual lives, however, the consequences can be much more devastating.

Near the end of the Sermon on the Mount, Jesus turned His attention to the reality of false teachers, whom He called false prophets. Jesus

71

described such people as "ferocious wolves," which highlights their purposes. False teachers aren't nice people who are a little confused. They aren't committed leaders who just need some extra direction.

No, false teachers are predators. They are out to destroy God's people and God's work in the world.

Thankfully, Jesus also taught us how to recognize false teachers. "By their fruit you will recognize them," He said. "Do people pick grapes from thornbushes, or figs from thistles? Likewise, every good tree bears good fruit, but a bad tree bears bad fruit" (Matt. 7:16–17). According to Jesus, the best way to avoid false teachers is to focus not on what they say but on what they do—on the fruit they produce through their lives and through their teaching.

The apostle Paul gave a little more insight into this idea of fruit: "But the fruit of the Spirit is love, joy, peace, forbearance, kindness, goodness, faithfulness, gentleness and self-control. Against such things there is no law" (Gal. 5:22–23). These are excellent measuring sticks to follow when evaluating spiritual leaders in your community and in your own spiritual life. Does that person demonstrate love? Peace? Do they show kindness and faithfulness? Are they self-controlled? Do they help produce that fruit in the lives of others, including your own?

Of course, the main way to be confident about spiritual teachers is to examine what they say about Jesus. "Who is the liar?" wrote the apostle John. "It is whoever denies that Jesus is the Christ. Such a person is the antichrist—denying the Father and the Son. No one who denies the Son has the Father; whoever acknowledges the Son has the Father also" (1 John 2:22–23).

Response

What dangers do false teachers pose within the church?

What are specific and practical ways you can evaluate spiritual leaders and their influence on your life?

SCRIPTURE MEMORY

The student is not above the teacher, but everyone who is fully trained will be like their teacher.

—LUKE 6:40

DAY 23

Jesus Taught About the Future

Because of the increase of wickedness, the love of most will grow cold, but the one who stands firm to the end will be saved. And this gospel of the kingdom will be preached in the whole world as a testimony to all nations, and then the end will come.
MATTHEW 24:12-14

It has become an all-too-common phenomenon in recent decades. I'm sure you've read about it several times in the news. A group of people flock around a leader who claims to have insider knowledge about the end of the world. The people sell their possessions. They liquidate their retirements. They gather together and wait for the end to come on a specific date.

And nothing happens. The specific day comes and goes with little fanfare.

I feel a deep sense of sadness whenever I hear stories about such cults. That's because the truth about the end of the world is available for anyone who cares to look for it. Specifically, they can find it in the sermon Jesus recorded in Matthew 24–25.

There are three key truths that Jesus taught about the future during that sermon. First, He made it clear there will be an end. "This gospel of the kingdom will be preached in the whole world as a testimony to all nations," Jesus proclaimed, "and then the end will come." This parade we know as human history is marching toward a final destination, a final confrontation. We are rushing our way toward not just a *when* but a *what*. The end.

Second, Jesus made it clear that the time and date and circumstances of that end are a mystery and will remain a mystery. "But about that day or hour no one knows," He taught, "not even the angels in heaven, nor the Son, but only the Father" (Matt. 24:36). Jesus compared those final moments with Noah's flood. People were out in the world eating and drinking, marrying and giving in marriage, clueless about what was coming their way. The same will be true at the end of history.

There are plenty of moments when Scripture carries a little mystery with it, but this is not one of them. Jesus' statements are plain and unmovable. Nobody knows when the end is coming, and nobody will know.

Third, and most important, Jesus emphasized many times that the reality of a coming end for our world means that we should stay focused. Be alert. Stay on our guard. "Therefore keep watch, because you do not know on what day your Lord will come" (v. 42). Jesus even illustrated this truth with a story in Matthew 25. He talked about ten virgins waiting up all night for a wedding party to arrive. All ten of the young women brought lamps to light the way for the wedding party, but only five brought oil. When the wedding party was delayed, the foolish five ran out of oil and were forced to go find more. While they were gone, the wedding party arrived and made its way to the groom's house. The five wise virgins joined the procession, but the other five were locked out.

The point of Jesus' story is brutally simple: Don't be left out. Don't get distracted by the world and miss what is most important. Stay focused on Jesus and actively do His will faithfully up to the day He comes.

Response

What have you heard or been taught about the end of the world?

Where are you in danger of losing focus or being distracted by things that don't have eternal significance?

SCRIPTURE MEMORY

The student is not above the teacher, but everyone who is fully trained will be like their teacher.

—LUKE 6:40

Jesus Taught Us to Be Faithful Stewards

Then the King will say to those on his right, "Come, you
who are blessed by my Father; take your inheritance, the
kingdom prepared for you since the creation of the world.
For I was hungry and you gave me something to eat, I
was thirsty and you gave me something to drink, I was a
stranger and you invited me in, I needed clothes and you
clothed me, I was sick and you looked after me, I was in
prison and you came to visit me."
MATTHEW 25:34-36

One of the things I like best about Jesus' teaching is the way He used
parables—short stories with a single, focused lesson. Parables are a
great way to illustrate specific truths, and Jesus used them brilliantly
throughout His ministry as a teacher.

There are two parables at the end of Jesus' sermon in Matthew 25
that are connected in a fascinating way. The first is the parable of the
talents, which is about a rich man who gave three servants different
amounts of gold before he departed on a long journey. He intended for
each servant to invest that gold while he was away so he could enjoy
the profits on his return. The first servant received five bags of gold,
and his investments produced five more. The second servant received
two bags of gold, and his investments produced two more. The third
servant received one bag of gold, but he refused to invest it, fearing

his master's wrath if he made a mistake. So he buried it and returned it to the master unchanged.

Unsurprisingly, the master was pleased with the work of the first two servants, and he rewarded them generously. But he was angry with the third, calling him a "wicked, lazy servant" (v. 26) and even commanding he be thrown "outside, into the darkness, where there will be weeping and gnashing of teeth" (v. 30).

The point of this parable is clear: God has entrusted each of us with a relative amount of resources. Most of us who are living in today's world, even if we aren't considered wealthy, have quite a lot of resources: time, money, talents, and so on. God expects us to be faithful stewards of those resources. He expects us to invest them in a way that produces a return for His kingdom.

What does that look like, though? What does it mean on a practical level to invest our resources in a way that makes a difference? That's where the second parable comes into play.

Jesus talked about a future moment when He returns as King and separates the world into two groups "as a shepherd separates the sheep from the goats" (v. 32). One group He will praise for serving Him by feeding the hungry, giving drink to the thirsty, showing kindness to strangers, clothing the naked, healing the sick, and visiting the prisoners. In the King's words, "Truly I tell you, whatever you did for one of the least of these brothers and sisters of mine, you did for me" (v. 40).

So as you sit down at the table with Jesus, remember He has work for you each day. Remember that you are His steward. He has called you and taught you to serve "the least of these" just as if you were serving Him.

Response

What are some resources God has entrusted to you and your household?

Where do you have opportunities to use those resources in a way that makes a difference for your community?

SCRIPTURE MEMORY

The student is not above the teacher, but everyone who is fully trained will be like their teacher.

—LUKE 6:40

SECTION 5

Jesus Is Our Great I Am

DAY 25

Jesus Is I Am

Thomas said to him, "Lord, we don't know where you are going, so how can we know the way?"

Jesus answered, "I am the way and the truth and the life. No one comes to the Father except through me."

JOHN 14:5-6

It's one of the most powerful moments in the entire Bible. When Moses turned aside to get a better look at something miraculous—a bush that was burning yet not consumed—he stumbled into a life-changing conversation with the Creator of the universe. During that conversation, Moses wanted to know God's name. He wanted to know who was sending him back into the dangerous teeth of Egypt and Pharaoh.

God's answer was both simple and profound: "I AM WHO I AM. This is what you are to say to the Israelites: 'I AM has sent me to you'" (Ex. 3:14).

Sit with that for a minute. Chew on it in your mind. Moses asked God's name, and God said, "I AM WHO I AM."

If you ever wonder about the nature of God, I AM WHO I AM sums things up wonderfully. God exists in an eternal present. He is and He will always be as He is. He is the Rock of existence, of reality, and every other thing or idea is defined by Him and through Him.

When you can wrap your mind around that, remember that Jesus is God. Jesus exists as this same being—He is I AM WHO I AM. It's appropriate, then, that Jesus used that phrase "I AM" to describe Himself on several occasions during His ministry on earth. We're

82

Jesus Is I Am

going to explore those moments over the next few days, but I think it's appropriate to start with Jesus' most comprehensive description of Himself: "I am the way and the truth and the life."

To set the context for this moment, Jesus had been describing heaven to His disciples. He'd just told them about His Father's house and that He was going there to prepare a place for those who follow Him. Not wanting to be left out, Thomas said, "Lord, we don't know where you are going, so how can we know the way?"

Jesus said, "I am the way." And this is where some people get a little uncomfortable, because Jesus didn't say "I am *a* way" or even "I am *the best* way." He spoke singularly. Definitively. He is *the* way to the Father. *The* way to salvation. *The* way to eternal life. Thankfully, we don't have to explain why that is true to a skeptical world. We simply need to point to Christ as the authority we follow.

Jesus is the way. Jesus is the truth. Jesus is the life. What's more, the Jesus sitting there at the table of your mind is the same Jesus who has always been at work in history, even before there was a history. He is the same yesterday, today, and forever.

Believing in I AM as you sit with Him at the table will bring you peace for every anxious moment.

Jesus has always been and will always be dependable, steady, and sure.

Response

When have you encountered God in a way that was especially powerful?

How can we communicate the reality of Jesus as *the* way in today's culture without being obnoxious or insulting?

SCRIPTURE MEMORY

Jesus answered, "I am the way and the truth and the life. No one comes to the Father except through me."

—JOHN 14:6

DAY 26

Jesus Is the
Bread of Life

**Then Jesus declared, "I am the bread
of life. Whoever comes to me will
never go hungry, and whoever believes
in me will never be thirsty."**
JOHN 6:35

I've eaten lots of different types of bread in my life (and enjoyed most
of them), but I've never eaten bread from heaven. To my knowledge,
that privilege has only been extended to the Israelites who wandered
in the wilderness after the exodus from Egypt.

It's a well-loved story. The Israelites didn't have the supplies necessary for their journey after leaving Egypt, and they let Moses know
about it: "If only we had died by the LORD's hand in Egypt! There we
sat around pots of meat and ate all the food we wanted, but you have
brought us out into this desert to starve this entire assembly to death"
(Ex. 16:3). Had I been there, I'm sure I would have been part of that
chorus of complaining.

God stepped in by providing huge masses of quail for the
Israelites to catch and eat that evening. The next morning, they
found an even more spectacular miracle: bread just lying on the
ground. Lots of bread. Tons of bread. And they found the same
thing morning after morning throughout their entire journey to the
promised land.

Fast-forward to Jesus' day, and you'll remember that Jesus accomplished a similar miracle by feeding five thousand men (plus women and children) by exponentially expanding five little barley loaves and two fish into a fantastic feast. Obviously, this was a big hit with the people. They were thrilled not just to see something miraculous but to receive a quality meal as part of the bargain.

Unfortunately, they weren't able to get past that specific miracle. When they encountered Jesus again, He tried to point them toward realities more important than hunger and bread. "Do not work for food that spoils," He said, "but for food that endures to eternal life, which the Son of Man will give you" (John 6:27).

Not getting the point, the people reminded Jesus of how Moses had given his followers manna, bread from heaven. "What sign then will you give that we may see it and believe you?" they asked. "What will you do? Our ancestors ate the manna in the wilderness" (vv. 30–31). Hint, hint.

Don't miss the truth here: The people wanted Jesus to fill their bellies while He was trying to nourish their souls. More than that, Jesus was trying to help them see their hunger not for food but for eternal life.

That's when Jesus laid everything on the line. "I am the bread of life," He declared. "Whoever comes to me will never go hungry, and whoever believes in me will never be thirsty." The Israelites had experienced God's provision of food, but here was Jesus—God in the flesh—offering something so much greater. Here was Jesus offering a life of satisfaction, fulfillment, and purpose. A life connected to Christ.

Will you take it and eat? The table is set. The offer is made. Jesus is the meal. And the choice is yours.

Response

When has God provided for you in a meaningful way?

What steps can we take to stop focusing on temporary things and instead concentrate on what is eternal?

SCRIPTURE MEMORY

Jesus answered, "I am the way and
the truth and the life. No one comes to
the Father except through me."

—JOHN 14:6

DAY 27

Jesus Is the Light of the World

When Jesus spoke again to the people, he said, "I am the light of the world. Whoever follows me will never walk in darkness, but will have the light of life."
JOHN 8:12

Why do we celebrate Christmas on December 25? Yes, there were some Christians living in the first centuries of the church who believed Jesus was actually born on that date, but nobody knew for certain. We still don't know for certain. The historical date of Jesus' birth is a mystery.

The reason the church selected December 25 as the day to celebrate Christmas is a little complicated, but it can basically be boiled down to one word: light. You see, the winter solstice occurs most commonly on December 21. In the Northern Hemisphere, that's the day when the earth's pole reaches its maximum tilt away from the sun, meaning that's the day with the least amount of sunlight each year.

Around the third century after Jesus' birth, different church councils determined that Christmas would be celebrated on December 25, just a few days after the winter solstice, a few days after the darkest night of the year. The symbolism was clear and powerful: Jesus' birth meant that the Light had entered the world.

John placed a heavy emphasis on the imagery of light at the beginning of his gospel, and rightfully so:

> In the beginning was the Word, and the Word was with God, and the Word was God. He was with God in the beginning. Through him all things were made; without him nothing was made that has been made. In him was life, and that life was the light of all mankind. The light shines in the darkness, and the darkness has not overcome it. . . .
> The true light that gives light to everyone was coming into the world. (1:1–5, 9)

Matthew also emphasized that theme at the beginning of his gospel, noting that Jesus' birth and ministry fulfilled a key prophecy from Isaiah 9:1–2: "The people living in darkness have seen a great light; on those living in the land of the shadow of death a light has dawned" (Matt. 4:16).

With all of that as background, Jesus understood exactly what He was doing when He declared, "I am the light of the world."

This world is a place of darkness. You don't need me to explain why that is true; you've seen it for yourself. But it's not just the world. We as human beings are filled with darkness. We are corrupted by the darkness of sin, and we spread that darkness over and over through our sinful actions. Left on our own, we are creatures of darkness and will always walk in darkness. That is precisely why we need the Light.

And once again, we don't just need it—we have it. *You* have it. The Light of the World is available to burn away the darkness, strengthen your perception, and bring clarity each and every day.

Response

Where do you see evidence of darkness in the world today?

Where do you see evidence of darkness in your own life?

SCRIPTURE MEMORY

Jesus answered, "I am the way and the truth and the life. No one comes to the Father except through me."

—JOHN 14:6

Jesus Is the Good Shepherd

Therefore Jesus said again, "Very truly I tell you, I am the gate for the sheep. All who have come before me are thieves and robbers, but the sheep have not listened to them. I am the gate; whoever enters through me will be saved. They will come in and go out, and find pasture. The thief comes only to steal and kill and destroy; I have come that they may have life, and have it to the full.

"I am the good shepherd. The good shepherd lays down his life for the sheep."

JOHN 10:7–11

James Rebanks is a modern-day shepherd. Working in the hills of Cumbria in northern England, Rebanks cares for hundreds of sheep on the same farm that has been in his family for more than six hundred years. He watches over the flock constantly, which is not an easy task in an area of the world known for harsh weather. He does whatever is necessary to keep each sheep in his charge safe, happy, and prosperous.

You could say that James Rebanks is part of an ancient tradition, and you would certainly be correct. But he has also brought a bit of modern technology to his profession. Specifically, social media. Rebanks is known on Twitter as the Herdwick Shepherd, and he regularly tweets musings and photographs to his 150,000 followers. He even wrote a memoir in 2015, *The Shepherd's Life*, which became an international bestseller.[1]

I appreciate people like James Rebanks because they help me understand Scripture on a different level. They open up a world that was common in ancient days but seems foreign or out of touch to most followers of Jesus today.

For example, when Jesus told His disciples, "I am the gate for the sheep," His statement had a specific meaning for them. They knew exactly what He was talking about, and they no doubt appreciated Jesus' ability to condense a complicated truth into a simple, powerful image.

Bible readers today need to do a little research, however, before we can fully understand what Jesus was communicating. For starters, we need to know that shepherds in the ancient world typically slept in the fields with their flocks to protect them from predators. Also, they usually herded their sheep into a small pen or enclosure that had four walls and a small gap that allowed the sheep to get in and out. However, instead of a gate, the shepherd himself laid across that gap, which meant nothing could get in or out without going through him.

In other words, the shepherd *was* the gate, which is exactly what Jesus communicated to His disciples. Jesus is the door through which we enter God's kingdom. He is the gate. And when we are part of His flock, there is nothing that can reach us or harm us or even touch us without going through Him. Therefore, we can "come in and go out, and find pasture." Moreover, we can "have life, and have it to the full."

Lastly, Jesus proclaimed, "I am the good shepherd"—another "I am" statement—and added, "The good shepherd lays down his life for the sheep."

That claim likely puzzled the disciples when they first heard it, but it doesn't puzzle us. Jesus gave His life so that we may have eternal life—eternal fellowship with Him. Why? Because He is the Good Shepherd—*your* Good Shepherd. He laid down His life for you.

Response

What are some occupations or images from today's world that would communicate something similar to "I am the gate for the sheep"?

How will you thank Jesus and praise Him for His role as your Good Shepherd?

SCRIPTURE MEMORY

Jesus answered, "I am the way and the truth and the life. No one comes to the Father except through me."

—JOHN 14:6

DAY 29

Jesus Is the Resurrection and the Life

Jesus said to her, "I am the resurrection and the life. The one who believes in me will live, even though they die; and whoever lives by believing in me will never die. Do you believe this?"

JOHN 11:25–26

Guests attending the funeral of Jorge Goncalves, a bricklayer from Brazil, received quite a shock when Jorge Goncalves himself walked into the service. Talk about a misunderstanding!

After a car crash late on a Sunday night, police believed the victim was Goncalves. The body was badly disfigured, but the clothes were similar to Goncalves's. Members of his family even identified the body. What they didn't realize is that Jorge had spent the night not on the road but at a truck stop, talking with friends. It's a tradition in Brazil to hold the funeral for a deceased person the day after they perish, so arrangements were made quickly. It wasn't until Monday that Goncalves heard what was going on and had the unique experience of attending his own funeral.[1]

There was no case of mistaken identity, however, when it came to Jesus raising Lazarus from the dead. Jesus heard that Lazarus was sick but chose not to rush immediately to His friend's bedside. Instead,

He lingered for a few days. He took His time. And when the disciples asked Him about it, Jesus replied, "Our friend Lazarus has fallen asleep; but I am going there to wake him up" (John 11:11).

When Jesus finally arrived in Bethany, Lazarus's sister Martha made no bones about her displeasure with his delay. "'Lord,' Martha said to Jesus, 'if you had been here, my brother would not have died'" (v. 21). When He told her confidently that her brother would rise again, she wasn't having it. "I know he will rise again in the resurrection at the last day," she said (v. 24). She thought Jesus was throwing a platitude her way, a phrase of useless comfort, and, like most people, she was not interested.

Then Jesus raised the stakes by making three statements that were beyond misunderstanding. First, He said, "I am the resurrection and the life." Once again, Jesus laid claim to the term "I am" to highlight His authority, His power. He was reminding Martha of His divine nature.

Second, He said, "The one who believes in me will live, even though they die." Jesus wanted Martha to see that physical death is not the final statement we often believe it to be. In fact, when we are connected to Christ, death is simply the passing between this life and a better version of this life. Death is just another part of eternal life.

Finally, Jesus declared, "Whoever lives by believing in me will never die." When we are made alive in Christ on a spiritual level, we are changed permanently. We are brought from spiritual death to spiritual life on a one-way ticket. No going back.

Jesus' final question to Martha was important for her, but it's also important for us. "Do you believe this?" If so, then take heart in the incredible gift you've been given! Use that truth to fortify your mind whenever the specter of death makes you feel afraid.

Response

How would you describe our culture's view of death?

What does it mean to believe in Jesus as described in John 11:25–26?

SCRIPTURE MEMORY

Jesus answered, "I am the way and the truth and the life. No one comes to the Father except through me."

—JOHN 14:6

DAY 30

Jesus Is the True Vine

I am the vine; you are the branches. If you remain in me and I in you, you will bear much fruit; apart from me you can do nothing.

JOHN 15:5

Have you ever had a chance to walk through a vineyard? It's an incredible experience. The vineyard's structure is stunning in and of itself—row after row, and trellis after trellis. The colors are astounding. And when the grapes are in season, you can't help reaching out to take hold of fruit that seems to be dripping deliciously from each vine.

When I read John 15, I like to picture Jesus walking with His disciples from Jerusalem to the Mount of Olives. I see Him passing by a grapevine, perhaps a vineyard or perhaps some wild fruit growing along the road, and stopping to observe. He motions for His disciples to gather round. They come close, hushed with the knowledge that the Teacher is about to teach.

"I am the true vine, and my Father is the gardener," He says (v. 1). I imagine Jesus taking the grapes in His hand, maybe holding one out for the disciples to see. He speaks of how the Father prunes away any branches that don't bear fruit, and He reminds the disciples that no branch can bear fruit by itself. In His words, "it must remain in the vine" (v. 4).

Then Jesus speaks the truth He has gathered them to hear: "I am the vine; you are the branches. If you remain in me and I in you, you will bear much fruit; apart from me you can do nothing."

It's that last statement that really shocks me when I think about it. I can't help thinking of myself as a competent person. I can't help thinking of myself as someone who can get things done. Someone who has resources and knows how to make the most of them. Someone who understands the value of hard work and is willing to do it.

In short, it's easy for me to believe I can accomplish things on my own. And not just silly things, either, but important things. Worthwhile goals.

Whenever I start to think that way, I know I need some time at the table with Jesus. Because the reality is Jesus was right: Apart from Him I can accomplish nothing of eternal significance. There is not a single thing of eternal value I can do or achieve based solely on my own strength, wits, or resources.

Why? Because I am a branch, not a vine. Every resource I have has been passed to me through the True Vine, Jesus, my Savior. And if I were to disconnect from that vine for even a moment, even a breath, I would wither. I would be useful only as fuel for the fire.

Please hear me: This isn't bad news. This isn't some expression of self-pity or self-loathing. It's just reality. And the more deeply I understand that reality, the more I will be able to remain in Jesus, the True Vine.

Response

How do you respond to the idea that you can accomplish nothing without a connection to Christ?

What does it mean to remain in Jesus as the True Vine?

SCRIPTURE MEMORY

Jesus answered, "I am the way and the truth and the life. No one comes to the Father except through me."

—JOHN 14:6

Jesus Is Lord of All

DAY 31

Jesus Is Lord

Therefore God exalted him to the highest place
and gave him the name that is above every name,
that at the name of Jesus every knee should bow,
in heaven and on earth and under the earth,
and every tongue acknowledge that Jesus Christ is Lord,
to the glory of God the Father.
PHILIPPIANS 2:9-11

Lord is a word we encounter all the time in church and in our Christian circles. We hear it in sermons. We hear it in prayers, both public and private. We read it in books and bulletins. We speak it. Sometimes we even shout it, maybe as an expression of praise or maybe as an exclamation of frustration. But what does that term actually mean? What are we saying when we use it? What should we be saying?

There's a sense in which that word can get lost in translation. When we hear the word *Lord*, a lot of us think of British aristocrats, especially as they are portrayed in TV shows. I'm talking about older men with puffy cheeks and powdered wigs and dressed in ridiculous outfits. Lord Perriweather of Dukeshire Falls or something like that.

That is not how the idea of *Lord* came across in the ancient world. Not at all. If you were the lord of something during Jesus' day, for example, you were a ruler. You were in charge. The buck stopped with you. That applied to a patriarch being lord of his household— both family and servants—all the way up to Caesar being lord of the Roman Empire.

In that context, the idea of lordship was connected with authority. Specifically, to be a lord was to demonstrate authority over a particular region or people or province. Lords made judgments. Lords set the rules. Lords gave orders and expected to be obeyed. That's what Scripture is communicating when it refers to Jesus as Lord. He carries authority. He *is* authority. We saw on day 6 that Jesus is supreme, that He is above all others. Paul pointed to that truth in Philippians when he wrote that Jesus is "exalted" to the "highest place," that His name is "above every name." This supremacy is the basis for Jesus' authority, for His Lordship.

Notice that the Lordship of Jesus is no small thing. He is exalted to such a level that "every knee should bow" and "every tongue acknowledge that Jesus Christ is Lord." Every being of every sort in heaven and on earth will eventually bow to the authority of Jesus. Every being of every sort in heaven and on earth will submit to His authority both physically and verbally because He is Lord.

What does that mean for you? Well, it means you are not Lord, not even a lord with a little *L*. But that's okay. You and I both know we would make terrible masters. That's why all of us should bow our knees and confess with our mouths that Jesus is Lord.

Response

Which people or organizations carry great authority in today's world?

What does it look like on a practical level to submit to Jesus' authority?

SCRIPTURE MEMORY

If you declare with your mouth, "Jesus is Lord," and believe in your heart that God raised him from the dead, you will be saved. For it is with your heart that you believe and are justified, and it is with your mouth that you profess your faith and are saved.

—ROMANS 10:9–10

Jesus Is Lord over Creation

In the beginning you laid the foundations of the earth,
and the heavens are the work of your hands.
PSALM 102:25

John Priest, known to history as the "unsinkable man," worked most of his life in the early 1900s as a fireman aboard steam vessels. He didn't put out fires; he stoked them. His job was to shovel coal into the massive boilers that powered massive seagoing ships. Unfortunately for John, the massive ships he worked on kept sinking under him!

Priest was working aboard HMHS *Asturias* when it collided with another vessel on its maiden voyage. He was aboard RMS *Olympic,* a sister ship of the *Titanic,* when it collided with the cruiser HMS *Hawke* in 1911. Then John got a job as a fireman on RMS *Titanic* in 1912, and we all know how that turned out. During World War I, he served on the merchant ship RMS *Alcantara,* which was sunk by a German raider in 1916. Finally, John joined the crew of HMHS *Britannic,* another sister ship of the *Titanic,* which struck a mine and sank near the Greek island of Kea, also in 1916.

Whew! Incredibly, John Priest survived all of those encounters and died in 1937—safely on land—of natural causes.[1]

Scripture describes another dangerous moment at sea in Luke 8. And while John Priest was not part of that voyage, there was still an unsinkable man on board: the Lord over creation.

It all started when Jesus said to His disciples, "Let us go over to the other side of the lake" (v. 22). The lake was the Sea of Galilee, a decent-sized body of water that typically would have taken three to five hours to cross. During the middle of the voyage, however, a fierce storm rose up and threatened the boat. Remember that several of Jesus' disciples were fisherman, so they knew how to handle themselves on the water. Even so, Scripture says, "the boat was being swamped, and they were in great danger" (v. 23).

Where was Jesus during this encounter? Sleeping, seemingly unaware of their peril. When the disciples woke Him up and cried out for help, He rebuked the winds and the waves. The storm calmed. Everything became peaceful. That's when the disciples asked their famous question: "Who is this? He commands even the winds and the water, and they obey him" (v. 25).

If those disciples had a better understanding of who Jesus is, they wouldn't have needed such a question. The Old Testament made it abundantly clear that Messiah, the Savior, would have authority over creation. As Psalm 102:25 declares, "In the beginning you laid the foundations of the earth, and the heavens are the work of your hands."

The psalmist was talking about Jesus, who is Lord over all creation. Jesus, who filled the sea to its depths and, to this day, both initiates and maintains the weather patterns that produce hot and cold, clear skies and clouds, cyclones and summer breezes. Jesus, who is master over every storm.

This means that you don't have to be some sort of unsinkable person; no matter what storm you're facing, the Lord over all creation is with you. He's got your back, and He's in charge.

Response

What are ways we can benefit from Jesus' authority over the natural world?

Where in your life does it feel like you're sinking? Why?

SCRIPTURE MEMORY

If you declare with your mouth, "Jesus is Lord," and believe in your heart that God raised him from the dead, you will be saved. For it is with your heart that you believe and are justified, and it is with your mouth that you profess your faith and are saved.

—ROMANS 10:9–10

DAY 33

Jesus Is Lord of the Sabbath

Then he said to them, "The Sabbath was made for man, not man for the Sabbath. So the Son of Man is Lord even of the Sabbath."
MARK 2:27-28

The Pharisees of Jesus' day loved rules. Loved them! They loved writing their own rules. They loved showing everyone else how well they followed their own rules. Unfortunately, they loved watching to make sure everyone followed their rules, and they loved coming down like thunder on those who failed to do so.

Now, to be clear, the Pharisees and the other religious leaders of Jesus' day weren't always focused on the rules of the Old Testament, which we sometimes call the Law. These were the six hundred or so commands God gave His people through Moses, and all of those commands are good. They reflect God's character and reveal the ways in which we fall short of His standard.

The problem came when the Pharisees and other religious leaders decided to interpret those laws by making more rules. Take the fourth commandment, for example: "Remember the Sabbath day by keeping it holy. . . . On it you shall not do any work" (Ex. 20:8, 10). That is a good commandment. It helps us understand the value of rest and of setting aside time to worship God.

But when God's people set about to follow that command, they hit a snag. Namely, what does it mean to work? Obviously, if I'm a blacksmith, I shouldn't do any smithing on the Sabbath. But could I plant a garden? Would that be work? Could I help my neighbor by shoeing his horse for free or would that be work? Which activities are defined as work and which are acceptable?

Not surprisingly, the Pharisees responded to this conundrum by making more rules. Many of them claimed, for example, that it was disobeying God to walk more than three-quarters of a mile on the Sabbath, because that could be considered work. Others said it was against God's law to spit on the ground on the Sabbath, because you might inadvertently water a seed, which would be farming. Therefore, work. Therefore, forbidden.

This was their mindset when they saw Jesus' disciples walking through a field one Sabbath day. Tragically, Scripture says those disciples "began to pick some heads of grain" (Mark 2:23). The Pharisees were shocked! This was a form of threshing, which was work. How could they! Indignantly, the Pharisees scolded Jesus, saying, "Look, why are they doing what is unlawful on the Sabbath?" (v. 24).

That's when Jesus reminded them of reality: "The Sabbath was made for man, not man for the Sabbath. So the Son of Man is Lord even of the Sabbath." Jesus told them the Sabbath was meant to be a gift. A time to find rest and peace and worship. A time to connect with almighty God. It was never meant to be a time for rules and restrictions and spiteful accusations.

How did Jesus know these things? Because "the Son of Man is Lord even of the Sabbath." Meaning that Jesus has authority over the Sabbath, because the Sabbath was a command from God, and Jesus is God. More than that, Jesus also has authority over those spiritual habits and religious rituals that so often start with good intentions but end up crowding out what's really important: our relationship with Him.

If you're feeling squeezed by traditions or the expectations of others, it might be time to let go of those things and focus on your connection with Jesus, who is Lord. In fact, it might be time to get some rest, both physically and spiritually. You don't need to work yourself into a religious stature. You don't need to earn anything from God. You just need to join Jesus at the table He's already set out for you. No doing—just being with Him.

Response

How have you typically approached the Sabbath? Why?

What are some traditions or religious expectations that make it more difficult for you to connect with God?

SCRIPTURE MEMORY

If you declare with your mouth, "Jesus is Lord," and believe in your heart that God raised him from the dead, you will be saved. For it is with your heart that you believe and are justified, and it is with your mouth that you profess your faith and are saved.

—ROMANS 10:9–10

Jesus Is Lord over the Grave

A week later his disciples were in the house again, and Thomas was with them. Though the doors were locked, Jesus came and stood among them and said, "Peace be with you!" Then he said to Thomas, "Put your finger here; see my hands. Reach out your hand and put it into my side. Stop doubting and believe."

Thomas said to him, "My Lord and my God!"

JOHN 20:26-28

It's hard to argue with a resurrection. After Jesus was crucified and buried in a tomb, His disciples were dismayed with confusion and grief. They didn't know what to do. They didn't know where to turn. They didn't understand how everything had turned so bad so quickly. That included Thomas.

Then, the morning of the third day, rumors started to fly. Women had visited the grave and found it empty. Peter and John had confirmed it. Then others started saying they had seen Jesus alive! Walking and talking and eating and breathing and laughing—all of it. Alive.

Thomas didn't see any of it, though. And Thomas wasn't about to believe something as far-fetched as a man rising from the grave without some evidence. "Unless I see the nail marks in his hands and put my finger where the nails were, and put my hand into his side," said Thomas, "I will not believe" (John 20:25).

That's where Jesus came in—literally. A week after Thomas's declaration, Jesus walked through a locked door and stood in front of him. "Put your finger here," He said. "See my hands. . . . Stop doubting and believe."

And to Thomas's credit, he did. I imagine him falling at Jesus' feet in both wonder and submission, gladness and shame. "My Lord and my God!"

As modern readers, it's important for us to understand that the resurrection of Jesus Christ is a historical event. It happened in the same way the Declaration of Independence happened. It was not some divine parlor trick. Jesus didn't flip a switch inside His brain that allowed Him to check out of Jerusalem for a few days and then check back in when things were more convenient. No, He died on that cross. His life drained away, and He experienced what every person has experienced when this life ends and the next begins.

Then, after death, He rose again. His body was filled with life once more. How is that possible? Simply because Jesus is Lord. Specifically, He is Lord over the grave. Jesus has authority over death. He is in charge of death, not the other way around. And through that authority, through that Lordship, Jesus conquered death on behalf of all people, including you and me.

Here's the truth: You are an eternal being. Yes, your body will one day cease to function, but that won't be the end of *you*. Not the real you. Just like Jesus, you will have a future even after you die. And when you are connected to Jesus, when you have accepted the gift of salvation purchased through His own death, that future is unbelievably bright.

So don't be afraid of death. Don't let it push you around. In fact, what better way to fortify your mind against the fear of death than to spend time each day at the table with Jesus, the Lord over the grave?

Response

What role has the fear of death played in your life so far?

How does Jesus' authority over death extend to you and your life?

SCRIPTURE MEMORY

If you declare with your mouth, "Jesus is Lord," and believe in your heart that God raised him from the dead, you will be saved. For it is with your heart that you believe and are justified, and it is with your mouth that you profess your faith and are saved.

—ROMANS 10:9-10

DAY 35

Jesus Is Lord over Evil

Jesus called his twelve disciples to him and gave them authority to drive out impure spirits and to heal every disease and sickness.

MATTHEW 10:1

Why did Jesus perform miracles? I chew on that question sometimes, even though I know there isn't any one correct answer. For example, we've already seen that Jesus is by nature a savior. So that was certainly a motivating factor when He encountered people in need.

I think another reason Jesus performed miracles during His public ministry was to demonstrate His authority over different aspects of life. Specifically, Jesus demonstrated authority over those areas of our lives that have been most deeply corrupted by sin, by the reality of evil in our world.

When you think about it, sickness and disease are directly connected to the corruption of sin, all the way back to the garden. Disease was never a part of God's plan for humanity, and if there were no sin, there would be no sickness. That's the reality of heaven. With our sin completely removed, we will find heaven to be a place with "no more death or mourning or crying or pain, for the old order of things has passed away" (Rev. 21:4).

With all that in mind, then, it's clear that each time Jesus healed someone, He was directly demonstrating His authority over the corruption and the consequences of sin. When Jesus healed the blind and told the paralyzed man to get up, take his mat, and walk, He showed

His Lordship over disability. When Jesus healed lepers and removed fevers, He showed His Lordship over disease. When Jesus took the hand of Jairus's daughter and said, *"Talitha koum!"* He showed His Lordship over death.

The same thing is true when Jesus confronted demons and cast them out. Notice that Jesus never tried to argue with demons or trick them into leaving those poor people alone. No, He rebuked them. He commanded them. He ordered them to be finished with their evil work, and they obeyed. Even the demons recognized Jesus' authority, His Lordship, and submitted to Him.

So Jesus is Lord over sin and the consequences of sin. He has authority over disease, death, and even demons. But that's not all. There's more to this theme, and it's even more astonishing.

In Matthew's Gospel, when we read about Jesus empowering His disciples, we see that Jesus not only had authority over the forces of evil and the consequences of sin in our world, but *He shared that authority with those who followed Him.* Jesus extended His Lordship out to His disciples and, through the window of history, to us.

Sometimes we don't realize how unusual that is. I mean, when you think back through the powerful men and women of history, can you think of any one of them who chose to share that power? Who gave away their authority, their lordship? I can't.

Yet that is the Lord we serve. That is the Lord who welcomes you to the table and gives you the power to take captive every thought in His name.

Response

How does our culture view the concept of evil?

What role do Christians have today in working against the forces of evil?

SCRIPTURE MEMORY

If you declare with your mouth, "Jesus is Lord," and believe in your heart that God raised him from the dead, you will be saved. For it is with your heart that you believe and are justified, and it is with your mouth that you profess your faith and are saved.

—ROMANS 10:9-10

Jesus Is Lord of Your Life

Suppose one of you has a servant plowing or looking after the sheep. Will he say to the servant when he comes in from the field, "Come along now and sit down to eat"? Won't he rather say, "Prepare my supper, get yourself ready and wait on me while I eat and drink; after that you may eat and drink"? Will he thank the servant because he did what he was told to do? So you also, when you have done everything you were told to do, should say, "We are unworthy servants; we have only done our duty."
LUKE 17:7–10

We've been focusing on the word *Lord* throughout this section as we continue diving more deeply into who Jesus is and how He works in our lives. We've seen that Jesus' Lordship is connected to His authority and to the reality that He is supreme: He is above all beings and in charge of all things.

Now I want to pivot a little and explore a word that is similar but carries a slightly different focus. That word is *Master*.

In my experience, it's one thing to recognize Jesus as Lord of all. It's relatively easy to acknowledge that Jesus is Lord over creation, Lord over spiritual practices and realities, Lord over death and the grave, and Lord over evil and its consequences. After all, each of those elements is out there. They are broad truths that can be pushed to the background of our lives if we choose to do so.

On the other hand, it's a much different thing to recognize Jesus as *Master*—specifically, to acknowledge that Jesus is *my* master. Doing so has a major effect on my life, because in order to recognize Jesus as my master, I need to acknowledge my own inferiority. I need to acknowledge my low position.

In short, if Jesus is Master, then I am His servant.

For many of us, this is where the rubber hits the road in our spiritual lives. After all, this is the twenty-first century. We're part of the modern world, surrounded and supported by fascinating technology. We're educated and have career ambitions. We've got dreams and goals. Every single day of our lives, our culture hammers us with the idea that we are the masters of our own fates, that we control our own destinies, for good or ill.

It's impossible to hold those ideas in one hand and grasp the truth of Jesus as Master in the other. Those realities cannot coexist. Either we are the masters of our lives or Jesus is.

Yet Jesus is not a hard-driving taskmaster. He is a servant-king. He came not to be served but to serve and to give His life as a ransom for all.

A master who chooses to serve is a master you can follow.

And what's more, His service sets you free.

Jesus isn't taking a vote. He is Lord and Master of all. When you join Him at the table, remember to show honor and to let Him know your desire is to do His will.

Response

What was your first response when you read Luke 17:7–10?

On a practical level, what does it mean to accept your role as a servant of Christ?

SCRIPTURE MEMORY

If you declare with your mouth, "Jesus is Lord," and believe in your heart that God raised him from the dead, you will be saved. For it is with your heart that you believe and are justified, and it is with your mouth that you profess your faith and are saved.

—ROMANS 10:9–10

Jesus Is Our Friend

DAY 37

Jesus Is Your Friend

You are my friends if you do what I command. I no longer call you servants, because a servant does not know his master's business. Instead, I have called you friends, for everything that I learned from my Father I have made known to you.
JOHN 15:14-15

Alan Robinson and Walter Macfarlane were born fifteen months apart in Hawaii. When they first met in sixth grade, they quickly became best friends and stayed that way. The two men developed a deep bond of friendship that allowed them to strengthen and support each other for more than sixty years.

Recently both men began researching their family histories through a DNA-matching website. Macfarlane never knew his father and Robinson was adopted, so each was interested in learning about their pasts and their family trees. You see where this is going, don't you? The tests showed both men had the same mother. After a lifetime of friendship, they learned they were actually brothers![1]

Like Alan and Walter, those of us who have a relationship with Jesus also have the benefit of knowing Him as both a friend and a brother.

Scripture says, "The Spirit you received brought about your adoption to sonship. And by him we cry, '*Abba*, Father.' The Spirit himself testifies with our spirit that we are God's children" (Rom. 8:15–16). This is a truly amazing benefit of salvation. Not only do we become citizens of God's kingdom, but we are adopted into God's family. We can call out to Him as Father. But then look at the next verse: "Now if we are children, then we are heirs—heirs of God and co-heirs with Christ, if indeed we share in his sufferings in order that we may also share in his glory" (v. 17). To be a child of God is also to be an heir, which means we are "co-heirs with Christ," who is the Son of God.

So in a very real sense, Jesus is your brother. Not your flesh and blood, of course, but your spirit and blood.

At the same time, Jesus is your friend. During the Last Supper, Jesus shared a great many truths and exhortations with His disciples. Among the most shocking was this statement: "I no longer call you servants, because a servant does not know his master's business. Instead, I have called you friends, for everything that I learned from my Father I have made known to you."

As we've seen throughout these pages, Jesus is far above all people and all beings. He is God. He is the Creator of all things. He is supreme in every way. He is Lord and Master.

And yet, there in that upper room, Jesus looked at those twelve men seated with Him—all of whom He had created, all of whom had stumbled and bumbled while following Him, and most of whom were about to abandon Him that same night—and He told them, "I have called you friends." What a statement! What a gift!

This is a critically important truth. Jesus seeks you out and offers a place at the table each day not because He has to and not because He is supposed to but because He wants to. Because He is your friend.

Response

What do you enjoy most about your closest friends?

How has Jesus been a friend to you?

SCRIPTURE MEMORY

Greater love has no one than this: to lay
down one's life for one's friends.

—JOHN 15:13

DAY 38

Jesus Loves You

**As the Father has loved me, so have I loved you. Now
remain in my love. If you keep my commands, you will
remain in my love, just as I have kept my Father's commands
and remain in his love. I have told you this so that my joy
may be in you and that your joy may be complete.**
JOHN 15:9–11

Most of us have heard the lyrics to that 1965 hit song about love. I
know, there are tons of songs out there about love, but I mean the one
that talks about what the world needs right now—not money, not
fame, and not even peace. Instead, what we need is love. Sweet love.
After all, according to the song, "It's the only thing that there's just
too little of."[1]

The good news is, as believers, you and I know the source of
love—all love—is our God. God doesn't just love; He is love. More
specifically, the God who is love both feels and expresses that love
toward you. God loves you.

But the question for you today is this: Do you believe it? Do you,
deep down, believe Jesus loves you?

I know the default answer is most likely yes. People within the
church feel obligated to respond, "Yes, I believe God loves me." But
saying something and knowing something are two very different
things. And right now I'm asking whether you know, really know
and believe at the core of who you are, that the God of all creation
loves you.

125

Sitting in a hospital room with my dad late in his life, I was floored when he told me that nobody in his life had ever loved him, and he didn't believe God could love him either. Those were the words of someone abandoned by his parents at an early age, someone who struggled to overcome the mountain of self-doubt all his life. Maybe that's where you are today, and it's hard to accept the fact that God cares about you, much less loves you.

If so, I need you to hear me and trust me, because what *you* need right now is love. God's love. No matter what circumstances have surrounded you, and no matter your opinion of yourself, it's important that you see Jesus went to great pains to show His love for you.

Look back to the Last Supper and you'll see Jesus made a promise to His followers: "As the Father has loved me, so I have loved you." That's an incredible statement, one you can't just let pass by. It needs to be front and center in your world every single day, starting today! The same love that existed between each person of the Trinity—Father, Son, and Spirit—also exists between God and you.

What that 1965 song proclaims is true: we all need love. Fortunately, the One you're at the table with *is* love. And even in this moment, He is extending that love to you.

Response

When have you experienced God's love in a meaningful way?

What does it look like for you to remain—to be rooted in the reality of—God's love?

SCRIPTURE MEMORY

Greater love has no one than this: to lay down one's life for one's friends.

—JOHN 15:13

DAY 39

Jesus Offers You Grace

For we do not have a high priest who is unable to empathize with our weaknesses, but we have one who has been tempted in every way, just as we are—yet he did not sin. Let us then approach God's throne of grace with confidence, so that we may receive mercy and find grace to help us in our time of need.

HEBREWS 4:15-16

We started yesterday's devotion by referencing a well-known pop song, but what would you say if I asked you which hymn was most loved in the global church? I'm guessing you'd say "Amazing Grace." If it's not your top pick, it's surely in the top three.

We love "Amazing Grace" because it is so poignant and powerful. The song was written from a deeply authentic place as the author, John Newton, under conviction from God, turned from being a slave trader to an abolitionist. He could truly say, "Amazing grace! how sweet the sound, that saved a wretch like me! I once was lost, but now am found, was blind, but now I see."[1]

Grace is often described as "unmerited favor," meaning we receive goodness and blessing we don't deserve. But the definition I like most for grace is a little more nuanced. Grace is *God at work*. It is God doing something I could not do myself.

On a practical level we see this unfold as grace becomes the vehicle through which we experience salvation. The message of the gospel

128

is that sin separates humanity from God. Too often we focus on the thought that sin makes us do bad things and, therefore, makes us bad people. But it's far worse than that. Scripture doesn't teach that sin makes us bad people; Scripture teaches that sin makes us spiritually dead people. And we know dead people cannot do anything to help themselves.

Yet, amazingly, Jesus stepped into our story through grace to do what we could not do for ourselves. Born without sin, Jesus was the only human fully and spiritually alive. Thus, when He took our sin onto His innocent life and died in our place, suffering the death we all deserve, Jesus made a way for us to be forgiven of all sin and to be brought from death to eternal life.

In other words, Jesus' death and resurrection represent a tremendous explosion of grace in our direction. We have been showered with unmerited favor by an act only Jesus could do. This is the foundation of our salvation and our lives; as the apostle Paul wrote, "For it is by grace you have been saved, through faith—and this is not from yourselves, it is the gift of God—not by works, so that no one can boast" (Eph. 2:8–9).

The most beautiful thing about God's amazing grace is that it's not designed just to get us to heaven. God's grace is available to get you through today. The same grace that brings us *to* life in Christ can also be accessed to get us *through* life in Christ.

As you join Jesus at the table today, take note of the scars on His wrists. Remember that you are no longer defined by your scars, but by His. Grace has exchanged your sinfulness for Jesus' righteousness. Therefore you can approach Him with confidence, right at His throne.

Breathe in grace and know that, just as Jesus was able to save you by grace, He can keep you by grace today.

Response

What benefits and blessings have you received because of Jesus' grace?

Where will you have an opportunity this week to extend grace to others?

SCRIPTURE MEMORY

Greater love has no one than this: to lay down one's life for one's friends.

—JOHN 15:13

Jesus Walks with You

Enoch was 65 years old when he fathered Methuselah. And after the birth of Methuselah, Enoch walked with God 300 years and fathered other sons and daughters. So Enoch's life lasted 365 years. Enoch walked with God; then he was not there because God took him.

GENESIS 5:21–24 HCSB

Can you imagine being on earth one minute and being mysteriously gone the next—not because you died, but because God gathered you up in His arms and you were instantly with Him?

That is exactly what happened to Enoch. It's one of the stories found in Scripture that has always arrested my thoughts and imagination.

What was it about Enoch that made him so special? Why did God decide to take him up? We know from other scriptures that Enoch was a faithful servant and a mighty prophet, even in the midst of a perverse generation. But what is most noteworthy about Enoch is that he walked with God even as he walked in this world.

The duality there is fascinating. Enoch was present within the corruption and pain and injustice of the world, yet he still walked with God. You know who else was able to balance that duality yet even more perfectly? Someone who was part of the world and yet still walked in perfect fellowship with God? That's right: Jesus.

It's been said that you can't understand someone until you've walked a mile in their shoes. Well, Jesus walked way more than a mile; He walked thirty-three years in human skin. He knows how hard life can be in a broken, sinful world. He knows how difficult it is to be part of that world and still remain connected to the Father.

But there's something even more startling to realize. Not only did Jesus walk *on earth* and face the same struggles you face, but Jesus wants to walk with you. It's why He created you, so you can know Him and make Him known. Like Enoch, God is inviting you to walk with Him. That means wherever your feet take you today, Jesus wants to walk with you.

Through the flood, He is there. In the fire of opposition, He's in lockstep. Up the mountain, He's climbing too. On a relaxing stroll on a sunny beach, Jesus is down for that. Through the valley of death, He says, "Fear not, for I am with you" (Is. 41:10 NKJV).

So how do we walk with Jesus and how do we know He is walking with us? Through the Holy Spirit who is living in us and leading the way. Paul wrote, "So I say, walk by the Spirit, and you will not gratify the desires of the flesh" (Gal. 5:16). Life is a series of steps, and those steps add up to your future. Invite Jesus into every step, every day. Nothing is too intimidating or too mundane for Him if you are there.

As you meet Jesus at the table today, remember He doesn't want to stay seated there when you get up to leave. Jesus is a good walking partner. He will walk you through today and every day. In fact, Jesus promises He will walk you all the way home.

Response

What do you find most difficult about being part of the world and still striving to remain connected with God?

Where do you especially need Jesus as your walking partner right now?

SCRIPTURE MEMORY

Greater love has no one than this: to lay down one's life for one's friends.

—JOHN 15:13

DAY 41

Jesus Befriends Sinners

For John the Baptist came neither eating bread nor drinking wine, and you say, "He has a demon." The Son of Man came eating and drinking, and you say, "Here is a glutton and a drunkard, a friend of tax collectors and sinners." But wisdom is proved right by all her children.
LUKE 7:33-35

There are 134 names or titles for Jesus throughout Scripture: *King of kings, Savior, Lord, God, Messiah.* All of them are great titles, but the one that intrigues me most is *friend of sinners*. It's likely not in the top tier of your list of titles for Jesus, but it should be.

I mean, aren't you glad Jesus is a friend of sinners?

Ironically, the name was given to Jesus by His religious adversaries, the Pharisees, who were teachers of the Law who strained for the appearance of outward righteousness and didn't cut any slack for the corrupt crowd—the sinners and tax collectors, the down and out, and the up and out. What the Pharisees meant as a slight, Jesus received and repeated about Himself, because He came into the world to save sinners and bring them to life again.

Jesus knew at the core of every person was a massive sin problem. He understood, "All have sinned and fall short of the glory of God" (Rom. 3:23). He was convinced every human ever born arrived in a sin condition that brought spiritual death.

That's true of you and me. We are all selfish. Sinful. Prideful. Doubt-filled. Strong-willed. We all are prone to wander from His path of truth and to do things our own way.

So who was Jesus supposed to befriend if not sinners? Who was He to eat with and hang out with if not sinners? Jesus was the only spiritually pure person on the planet during His entire lifetime.

Unlike the Pharisees, Jesus didn't despise sinners. He loved them. And that's still true for you and me. Make no mistake, Jesus is diametrically opposed to sin—so much so that He stepped into our world to crush its power over our lives by being crushed Himself in our place on the cross. He did this not because He hates you, but because He loves you. And He loves your classmate, your coworker, your neighbor, your family member, and even those whose lives are a tangled, sinful mess, the ones who seem far, far away from God. And, yes, He loves even those who are hostile to Him.

How is Jesus going to love them? He wants to love them through *you*. He wants you to be not just His hands and feet but His heart. Of course, He doesn't want to put you in harmful relationships or situations because you are trying to remain focused on the mission. The Scripture calls us to be in the world but not of the world.

Still, Jesus wants to walk across the street with you and into the lives and stories of those around you.

Your Enemy, however, wants to convince you that Jesus could never like you. Not with all your blemishes. Not with all your failures.

Don't listen to those lies! Jesus invites you—a rebel turned son or daughter—to the table, and He wants you to invite others to know they have an invitation to dine with Him.

Response

What makes you feel unworthy of a connection to Christ?

What are specific ways we can reach out to Jesus and accept His offer of friendship?

SCRIPTURE MEMORY

Greater love has no one than this: to lay down one's life for one's friends.

—JOHN 15:13

DAY 42

Jesus Will Never Leave You

**Keep your lives free from the love of money and be content
with what you have, because God has said,**

> **"Never will I leave you;
> never will I forsake you."**

HEBREWS 13:5

Some of the most difficult times in life are when we experience someone leaving. Even kids discover what that feels like when their friends move away or move on to another friendship. Dating and relationships can be a wonderful adventure, but many are also filled with loss. By the time we get a little older, most of us have had brushes with death. Losing anyone we care about is never easy, and sometimes we start to wonder whether there's anything we can depend on, whether there's anyone we can depend on.

Will everyone I love wind up leaving me?

That's the voice of the Enemy speaking. The reality is there is one relationship you can always count on. There is one friend you will never be parted from, not even for a moment. That friend is Jesus, who made you this promise: "Never will I leave you; never will I forsake you."

You wonder, *How can that be? I've never seen Jesus, so how is He with me?* The answer is the Holy Spirit. To see what I mean, let's take

137

one more look at Jesus' conversation with His disciples at the Last Supper.

Prior to His arrest and crucifixion, Jesus prepared His disciples for what was coming by teaching them about the Holy Spirit. "I will ask the Father, and he will give you another advocate to help you and be with you forever," He said, "the Spirit of truth" (John 14:16–17). Jesus said the world would never understand the Holy Spirit, because it neither sees Him nor knows Him. Then the Lord made this incredible statement: "But you know him, for he lives with you and will be in you" (v. 17).

That's critical. The Holy Spirit lives in you. And because that Spirit is part of the Trinity—because that Spirit is God—then Jesus is permanently connected to you through His Spirit. He said: "Before long, the world will not see me anymore, but you will see me. Because I live, you also will live. On that day you will realize that I am in my Father, and you are in me, and I am in you" (vv. 19–20).

The long and the short of these promises is that God is eternally connected with all who experience His salvation. The Spirit lives inside us and permanently connects us to both the Father and the Son. That connection is unshakable.

Now, having said that, there will certainly be times in our lives when we *feel* as if God is far away. There will be times when it seems as if we can't hear His voice or discern His presence. But in those moments, Jesus encourages us to come closer to Him, to scoot in our chairs as close to the table as we can. Then we will experience His love and encouragement so we can fortify our minds with the truth of Jesus' promise: "Never will I leave you; never will I forsake you."

Response

How do you typically respond when it feels as if God is distant or unreachable?

What are some practical steps you can take to actively seek out God's presence and listen for His voice?

SCRIPTURE MEMORY

Greater love has no one than this: to lay
down one's life for one's friends.

—JOHN 15:13

Jesus Leads His Church

DAY 43

Jesus Is Head of the Church

He is before all things, and in him all things hold together. And he is the head of the body, the church; he is the beginning and the firstborn from among the dead, so that in everything he might have the supremacy.
COLOSSIANS 1:17–18

The oldest church building in the world is called the Dura-Europos church. Situated in Syria, it was originally constructed somewhere around AD 230, just two centuries after the death and resurrection of Jesus! Dura-Europos has been unused for centuries, but archaeologists believe the building was first constructed as a private home before it became a church. That's appropriate since most Christians who worshiped in those early centuries did so at house churches.

If you want to find the oldest church building still in use, that's probably the Monastery of Mar Sarkis, which is also in Syria. Constructed during the early fourth century, Mar Sarkis has been in operation as a convent, monastery, and gathering place for more than seventeen centuries. That's almost seven times longer than the United States has been a nation![1]

There's a word I keep using when I describe these structures, and I'm using it intentionally. That word is *building*. Whenever we think about a church, it's critical to remember what it is and what it is not.

142

Specifically, church buildings are not the church. Dura-Europos and Mar Sarkis are churches, yes, but not *the church*. The same is true for St. Peter's Basilica in Rome or Westminster Abbey in London. The same is true for Passion City Church in Atlanta and Washington, DC. The same is true from the First Baptist Church of Middletown, America, all the way to Chinese house churches meeting secretly in basements and everywhere in between.

The church is not a building or a collection of buildings. Instead, the church is people.

More specifically, the church is the collected gathering of individuals who have experienced the salvation of Jesus Christ both now and throughout history. That's important. What we call the church isn't limited to human beings who are walking and talking today, at this moment. The church encompasses every follower of Christ from every period of human history—past, present, and future.

This collection of individuals is what we often refer to as *the body of Christ*. And at the head of that body is Christ Himself. Jesus is the Head of the church.

What does that mean? We're going to explore that question over the next few days, but the basic idea is that Jesus operates within the church the same way your head operates within your body. Jesus is the brains of the outfit. His mind and will established the church and hold it together. He is in charge.

Unfortunately, there are times when your body does things your head doesn't want it to do. Think about sickness, clumsiness, aging, and so on. In the same way, there have been many times throughout history—and there are many, many times each day—when the body of Christ fails to do what the Head has commanded.

Even so, we are called to press forward as the church and continue to carry out Jesus' work and His will, which requires us to fortify our minds even as we seek to obey His mind. It requires us to consistently defer to Christ as the Head of the church.

Response

What words would you use to describe your recent experiences in church buildings?

How would you describe or summarize your place in the church?

SCRIPTURE MEMORY

Now you are the body of Christ, and
each one of you is a part of it.

—1 CORINTHIANS 12:27

DAY 44

Jesus Set the Mission for the Church

Then Jesus came to them and said, "All authority in heaven and on earth has been given to me. Therefore go and make disciples of all nations, baptizing them in the name of the Father and of the Son and of the Holy Spirit, and teaching them to obey everything I have commanded you. And surely I am with you always, to the very end of the age."
MATTHEW 28:18–20

Military leaders often refer to an idea called *commander's intent*, which is the overall objective for a specific mission or even for an entire battle. Say a general wants to retake a city that is occupied by terrorists. The general would give specific orders to specific troops. "First platoon, target this area. . . . Second platoon, secure these streets. . . . Third platoon, take out these artillery installments." He issues several specific orders, but all of them are part of a single primary objective: capture and secure the city. That is the commander's intent.

The reason this is important is because what military leaders plan to happen doesn't always line up with what actually happens. In fact, it often doesn't. A group might be given a mission to secure a specific building, but when they arrive on scene, they find that building has been destroyed. What then? The platoon leader would think, *The commander's intent is to capture this city, so what can we do to contribute to that objective?*

I bring all of this up because what we find at the end of Matthew 28 is Jesus' commander's intent for the church. It's the overall objective Jesus has called us to accomplish as His body. Actually, more than called. It's what He has *commanded* us to accomplish as His body.

Notice that Jesus' command began with an affirmation of His authority: "All authority in heaven and on earth has been given to me. Therefore . . ." As we've already seen in these pages, Jesus is Lord. He is supreme. He is the commander, and He gave these orders based on that authority.

What are the orders, then? Let's look at the verbs: "go," "make disciples of all nations," "baptizing them," "teaching them." That's our mission as the church, as the body of Christ.

Of course, we do have specific orders as well. Christians all around the world have been intentionally planted in specific communities to accomplish specific goals on behalf of Christ. Jesus guides the circumstances of our lives. He brings people into our spheres of influence for specific reasons. He has specific work for us to do each day.

Still, there will be moments in our lives when we are unsure of exactly what Jesus is calling us to accomplish on His behalf. The good news is that we don't have to flounder in those moments. We don't have to wait for a neon sign or a lightning bolt to get us moving. Instead, we can focus on the commander's intent given to us by Christ. We can go into our communities. We can actively look for opportunities to make disciples. We can baptize those who have responded to God's call. And we can continually seek out moments to teach those who are ready to learn.

Response

What specific goals or directions is Jesus calling you to accomplish this week?

When you look at your life through the lens of the Great Commission in Matthew 28, what do you see?

SCRIPTURE MEMORY

Now you are the body of Christ, and
each one of you is a part of it.

—1 CORINTHIANS 12:27

Jesus Sets the Example for the Church

To the elders among you, I appeal as a fellow elder and a witness of Christ's sufferings who also will share in the glory to be revealed: Be shepherds of God's flock that is under your care, watching over them—not because you must, but because you are willing, as God wants you to be; not pursuing dishonest gain, but eager to serve; not lording it over those entrusted to you, but being examples to the flock. And when the Chief Shepherd appears, you will receive the crown of glory that will never fade away.

1 PETER 5:1–4

People have a lot of misconceptions about pastors in the church today. Of course, one of the big ones is that pastors work only one day a week. Ha! Another misconception is that pastors always have it together and always feel confident in themselves, in their spiritual lives and in the work they do. I can tell you from personal experience that's not the case. Pastors have most of the same challenges that plague everyone else within the church.

The most damaging misconception people often have about pastors is that we are the leaders of the church. This is especially true within specific congregations. For example, there may be people who attend Passion City Church, where I serve, who believe I am the leader of our church. Sadly, I know there are pastors out there who would echo that sentiment, pastors who believe they are the leaders of their churches.

Here's the reality: Jesus is the leader of the church. Full stop. Period. End of sentence. As we've already seen, He is the Head. He is in charge. He sets the agenda and fuels everything that is accomplished by the church and within the church.

Really, that's the hierarchy established in Scripture. That's exactly what the apostle Paul was describing when he wrote, "Follow my example, as I follow the example of Christ" (1 Cor. 11:1). Paul acknowledged his role as a leader, and he declared his desire to live and work as an example for others within the church. But the basis for Paul's leadership was his own decision to follow Jesus. Meaning, Jesus is the leader, Paul was a follower, and Paul was willing to serve as an example for his fellow followers.

Peter gave the same instructions in 1 Peter 5. He acknowledged that Jesus is the "Chief Shepherd." He is the Head of the church. He sets the agenda. Then Peter instructed the elders in the church—those with leadership roles in different congregations—to be "examples to the flock." Namely, Peter wanted the small-*S* shepherds in the church to emulate the example of the Chief Shepherd. To watch over the flock. To care for them. To resist every impulse toward greed or pride or apathy.

That's where you and I come in. All of us have influence we can invest in the lives of others. All of us have a mission to make disciples, to go and baptize and teach. Which means all of us—you, me, and every disciple of Jesus Christ—have a responsibility to shepherd those whom God has placed around us.

The good news is we can! You can. You can lead those around you simply by following the example of Jesus, your Good Shepherd.

Response

Who is following your spiritual example right now?

Where are you currently falling short of the example set by Christ?

SCRIPTURE MEMORY

Now you are the body of Christ, and
each one of you is a part of it.

—1 CORINTHIANS 12:27

Jesus Unites the Church as His Body

Just as a body, though one, has many parts, but all its many parts form one body, so it is with Christ. For we were all baptized by one Spirit so as to form one body—whether Jews or Gentiles, slave or free—and we were all given the one Spirit to drink. Even so the body is not made up of one part but of many.

1 CORINTHIANS 12:12-14

The human body is fascinating in part because it is incredibly complex. In fact, our bodies are so complex we are still discovering new things about ourselves every year. We're even discovering new organs!

In 2018, scientists discovered a new organ called the interstitium. It exists just below your skin and is structured as a mesh. We still don't know exactly what this organ does, but it probably acts as a kind of shock absorber, especially for all our other organs. The reason the interstitium had gone undetected for so long was because scientists usually dehydrate slides and samples before looking at them under microscopes, and this new organ is filled with fluid.[1] Then, incredibly, scientists discovered another new human organ just two years later! Now known as tubarial salivary glands, they exist behind the nose, hidden for centuries within the cartilage there. Their primary function seems to be to lubricate the nose and upper throat.[2]

Think about how many doctors and other researchers study the human body every day. Think about how many patients have been poked and prodded and cut and stitched up over the centuries. And yet our bodies are so intricate and so incredibly designed that we are still discovering new parts and pieces.

Just as the human body is complex, so, too, is the body of Christ. I have the privilege of traveling regularly, and I love the experience of doing church in other countries and other cultures. There is an incredible beauty in witnessing the astonishing diversity of Jesus followers around the globe.

People from different cultures may express their worship in different ways. I've been in cultures where all the people break out in dancing, and others who appear more reserved, with no one so much as offering a loud "amen." And people from differing cultures approach the mission of reaching their corner of the world by different means.

Though we hold to the same scriptural teachings and confess Jesus as Lord, there are differing tastes, different expressions, and different styles throughout the world and, most likely, within your own church.

Still, despite the differences and diversity within the church, we are unified. Specifically, we are unified by Jesus. We make up many parts, but we are all gathered by Christ into a single body, a single church.

As a follower of Jesus, you are a part of that body. You are a member of that church. Which means you have a responsibility to seek unity with other Christians, even and especially with other Christians who are different from you. Doing so not only benefits you, but it also brings glory and honor to Jesus followers with different styles, tastes, and backgrounds than yours.

Response

What are some consequences of divisions and disunity within the church?

Where do you see churches or groups of Christians that are doing a good job of striving for unity?

SCRIPTURE MEMORY

Now you are the body of Christ, and
each one of you is a part of it.

—1 CORINTHIANS 12:27

153

DAY 47

Jesus Equips the Church

So Christ himself gave the apostles, the prophets, the evangelists, the pastors and teachers, to equip his people for works of service, so that the body of Christ may be built up until we all reach unity in the faith and in the knowledge of the Son of God and become mature, attaining to the whole measure of the fullness of Christ.
EPHESIANS 4:11-13

Our world learned a lot about itself during the COVID-19 pandemic. We learned a lot about who we are, how we respond to pressure-filled situations, and how we tend to communicate during difficult times. Some of those lessons were good, and many were not so good.

One of the biggest lessons we learned as a society is that we need to be much more thankful for the women and men who keep us equipped with all the necessities of life. I'm talking about factory workers. I'm talking about truck drivers, both long- and short-haulers. I'm talking about midnight grocery stockers and courageous cashiers. These people and many others are essential in equipping and fueling our culture so it can run as efficiently as possible.

Looking to the church, it's clear from Scripture that it takes a lot of resources for the body of Christ to fulfill its mission in the world. It takes a lot of fuel to keep this train running on the tracks. And what we need to remember is that those of us within the church don't provide those resources ourselves; we don't provide that fuel.

Instead, Jesus equips the church with everything necessary to carry out His work.

That includes people, as Paul made clear: "So Christ himself gave the apostles, the prophets, the evangelists, the pastors and teachers, to equip his people for works of service." Without a doubt, people are the church's greatest resource. And people are the primary vehicle through whom Jesus accomplishes His work.

Do you see the progression there? Jesus equips leaders to minister within His church, and those leaders then equip the church itself "for works of service."

In another letter to the church, Peter taught that Jesus' "divine power has given us everything we need for a godly life through our knowledge of him who called us by his own glory and goodness" (2 Peter 1:3). He added,

> For this very reason, make every effort to add to your faith goodness; and to goodness, knowledge; and to knowledge, self-control; and to self-control, perseverance; and to perseverance, godliness; and to godliness, mutual affection; and to mutual affection, love. For if you possess these qualities in increasing measure, they will keep you from being ineffective and unproductive in your knowledge of our Lord Jesus Christ. (vv. 5–8)

Jesus equips His people with "everything we need." That includes physical resources, such as money, but it also includes immaterial resources, such as goodness, knowledge, self-control, perseverance, godliness, and love. All these tools are necessary to carry out our work within the church. And all these tools are provided by Christ.

Remember that truth as you sit at the table with Jesus. He has equipped you with many resources, and He has done so for a reason: "that the body of Christ may be built up."

Response

What resources has Jesus equipped you with?

Where do you see opportunities to use those resources within your congregation and community?

> **SCRIPTURE MEMORY**
>
> Now you are the body of Christ, and
> each one of you is a part of it.
>
> **—1 CORINTHIANS 12:27**

DAY 48

Jesus Preserves His Church

Simon Peter answered, "You are the Messiah, the Son of the living God."

Jesus replied, "Blessed are you, Simon son of Jonah, for this was not revealed to you by flesh and blood, but by my Father in heaven. And I tell you that you are Peter, and on this rock I will build my church, and the gates of Hades will not overcome it."

MATTHEW 16:16–18

In April 2019, the world watched in horror as Notre-Dame de Paris caught fire. The iconic cathedral had stood proudly at the center of Paris for more than 850 years, but all of a sudden admirers from every nation were confronted with the very real possibility that Notre-Dame could be destroyed.

Thankfully, much of the cathedral was saved by firefighters and emergency crews. Still, the church suffered heavy damage. The roof—itself a work of art—was the central location of the fire, and it was completely destroyed. The cathedral's iconic spire, constructed from 500 tons of wood and 250 tons of lead, collapsed beyond repair. Many important relics and works of art were damaged or destroyed. Thankfully, no lives were lost during the blaze.[1]

As I mentioned at the beginning of this section, church buildings are not the church. It's people who make up the body of Christ.

Yet it's important to recognize that the church as an institution can come under attack. In fact, the church *is* under attack and has *always* been under attack by the forces of evil in this world. And just as the cathedral of Notre-Dame was saved by the courageous efforts of emergency workers, the church as an institution is continually saved, protected, and preserved by the power of Jesus Christ.

Matthew 16 offers an interesting moment in Jesus' public ministry because it's one of the rare times when Jesus acknowledged His status as Messiah, the Christ. Or, in Peter's words, "You are the Messiah, the Son of the living God."

But then Jesus made two important statements regarding the church. First, He said, "I tell you that you are Peter, and on this rock I will build my church." It's easy to go off into the weeds arguing about what rock Jesus was referring to, but we need to highlight the promise Jesus made in that moment: *"I will build my church."*

Jesus spoke definitively in that moment. No matter what comes or what enemies align against Him, Jesus will build His church. Notice that participle "my." Jesus didn't say He would build "a church" or "the church" but "my church." He takes ownership of the institution.

His second statement is just as powerful: "and the gates of Hades will not overcome it." This is another promise we can take to the bank. No matter what enemies array themselves against the church, they will not prevail. No matter what forces seek to undermine the church— whether from within or without—those forces will fail.

As the world marches inexorably toward the end of history, sooner or later Notre-Dame will fall. Our worship buildings at Passion City Church, like all local churches, will crumble into dust. Ministry organizations will rise and fall and rise and fall again. But through it all, the church will remain. Through it all, the church will stand as a testimony to the faithfulness of Jesus Christ.

Equally important, the church is standing now, and you are part of it. You are part of the body of Christ, and you have work to do on

His behalf. So fortify your mind in the truth that Jesus will preserve you and support you and bless you even as He has preserved and supported and blessed His church.

Response

What are some ways you have seen the church suffer attacks from its enemies?

In what ways are you currently benefiting from the church? In what ways are you contributing?

SCRIPTURE MEMORY

Now you are the body of Christ, and
each one of you is a part of it.

—1 CORINTHIANS 12:27

Jesus Is Our Way to the Father

DAY 49

Jesus Is Our High Priest

For this reason he had to be made like them, fully human in every way, in order that he might become a merciful and faithful high priest in service to God, and that he might make atonement for the sins of the people. Because he himself suffered when he was tempted, he is able to help those who are being tempted.

HEBREWS 2:17-18

Take a moment to think about those items in your household that were special when you were a child. I'm talking about the couch you were never allowed to jump on. Or maybe it was a set of china that was only used on holidays or when important guests joined your family for a meal. Or maybe your family had some heirlooms hanging on the walls that were passed down from previous generations, which is why you weren't allowed to throw anything in the house.

Can you think of those special objects? I mention them because I want to call out the idea of something being set apart, being reserved for a special purpose and a special function. In many ways, that's how Scripture communicates and illustrates the role of a priest in the ancient world.

The book of Leviticus explores how God established the sacrificial system for His people, the Israelites. The whole book is a fascinating read filled with powerful imagery and symbolism, but I want to focus for a moment on the day when God, through Moses, ordained the first priests to work within that system. When you read through

Leviticus 8, you see Moses sacrifice a bull and two rams. Then he spent an entire day consecrating different articles to be used for God's service: the tabernacle, the altar, the different tools and elements used for sacrifices, and so on. Moses sprinkled all of these with the blood of the bull and the rams as a way to set them apart. To ordain them. To make them holy.

Moses did the same thing with those first priests: "Then Moses took some of the anointing oil and some of the blood from the altar and sprinkled them on Aaron and his garments and on his sons and their garments. So he consecrated Aaron and his garments and his sons and their garments" (Lev. 8:30).

If you've ever tried to wash oil out of clothes, you know it's tough. If you've ever tried to wash blood out of something, you know it's almost impossible. And that was exactly the point! Just as a special red plate is set apart from the rest of your tableware, the priests were set apart from the rest of the Israelites. They were ordained by the blood. Made holy.

The book of Hebrews goes to great lengths to show how the same is true of Jesus. He is our "merciful and faithful high priest in service to God." Jesus was and is set apart for a special role, a special purpose. Ordained. Made holy. And He was set apart through the shedding of His own blood.

Now here's the best part. The priests of the Old Testament were not only set apart for service to God, but they were also largely set apart from their community in a practical sense. They had their own homes. They spent most of their working time at the temple. They were largely distant from regular people, common folk.

Not Jesus. Your High Priest is right beside you. Never far off. Never distant. He stands with you to fortify your mind, strengthen your heart, and keep you strong in your faith.

Response

What are some tools or objects in your home that are set apart for a specific function?

Why are Jesus' sufferings and humanity an important element in His role as High Priest?

SCRIPTURE MEMORY

For there is one God and one mediator between God and mankind, the man Christ Jesus, who gave himself as a ransom for all people.

—1 TIMOTHY 2:5-6

DAY 50

Jesus Is the Mediator Between God and Humanity

This is good, and pleases God our Savior, who wants all people to be saved and to come to a knowledge of the truth. For there is one God and one mediator between God and mankind, the man Christ Jesus, who gave himself as a ransom for all people. This has now been witnessed to at the proper time.

1 TIMOTHY 2:3-6

As we continue to explore the reality that Jesus is the High Priest within the kingdom of God, I want to acknowledge that the word *priest* has a lot of different connotations and associations in today's world. Some people hear this word and think of old men in ornate robes. For others, it evokes feelings of somberness and seriousness. Of course, some associate it with silliness or even superstition. And, tragically, there are too many for whom the word *priest* brings up memories of abuse, shame, and trauma.

For this discussion, however, it's important that we focus specifically on a biblical understanding of the priesthood. As we saw yesterday, the priests described in Scripture were set apart for service to God. They were made holy.

You might be wondering, *Set apart for what? What did the priests actually do?* The answer points to the second reality about priests in the Bible: they primarily operated as mediators between God and humanity. More specifically, they interceded with God on behalf of the people by fulfilling God's requirements for the forgiveness of sin.

I know—there's that word again: *sin.* As we saw earlier, all people are corrupted by sin, which is why all people begin their lives in a state of separation from God. Sin cuts us off from the relationship with God we were all created to enjoy, to need.

That's where the priests came in. The Old Testament shows how priests were set apart within their community for the specific function of dealing with sin. They helped people offer the sacrifices God required to make an atonement for their sin, to be forgiven. Of course, these sacrifices were imperfect because they were offered by imperfect people. That's why everyone, the priests included, had to continue making those sacrifices year after year.

That's where Jesus comes in. Like the priests of the Old Testament, Jesus was set apart to help humanity deal with the problem of sin. He is a mediator between God and people. He works on our behalf.

Unlike the priests of the Old Testament, Jesus is unstained by sin. As we've seen throughout these pages, He is pure. Supreme. Fully God even as He is fully man. Therefore, when Jesus steps in as the mediator on our behalf, He does so perfectly. He completely bridges the gap of separation that exists between humanity and God.

The Enemy, however, wants you to believe that God is somewhere on the far edges of the universe. Distant. Aloof. Uncaring. Of course, that is a lie.

The truth is that Jesus is constantly working to bring you into a deeper connection with Himself. With God. Jesus is constantly interceding on your behalf, because He is your mediator and the Great High Priest.

Response

Where do you see mediators at work within society today?

Why is it critical to understand there is only one mediator between God and us?

SCRIPTURE MEMORY

For there is one God and one mediator between
God and mankind, the man Christ Jesus, who
gave himself as a ransom for all people.

—1 TIMOTHY 2:5-6

DAY 51

Jesus Is Our Atonement

For all have sinned and fall short of the glory of God, and all are justified freely by his grace through the redemption that came by Christ Jesus. God presented Christ as a sacrifice of atonement, through the shedding of his blood—to be received by faith.
ROMANS 3:23-25

I said earlier that the book of Leviticus is packed with rich and powerful symbolism, and chapter 16 describes the first instance of what we know as the Day of Atonement, or *Yom Kippur*. On that day, the high priest was charged with carrying out several rituals and sacrifices designed to atone for himself and for the community.

The literal translation of the word *atonement* in Hebrew is "covering," and in connection with these sacrifices it carries the idea of being covered by blood. When an animal's blood was shed, that sacrifice covered the sins of the people. So, on a practical level, atonement means a price has been paid to achieve forgiveness.

On the Day of Atonement, the high priest made sacrifices and participated in ritual washings and other ceremonies that were common for the Old Testament sacrificial system. But there's one element of the rituals I find especially fascinating, and it involved two goats. The first goat was sacrificed, and its blood was sprinkled on the ark of the covenant. But the second goat had a different path. The high priest was "to lay both hands on the head of the live goat and confess over it all the wickedness and rebellion of the Israelites—all their sins—and put them on the goat's head" (Lev. 16:21). Then the goat was released in a remote part of the wilderness to carry the sins of the people far away. (This ritual is where we get the term *scapegoat*, by the way.)

The reason I find this ritual with the two goats so fascinating is that both elements point to the death of Jesus. First, Jesus is like the scapegoat in that He took the sins of humanity upon Himself. And not just the sins of His local community, but the whole world. And not just the sins of the people in His day, but the sins of every human who has ever lived or will ever live. And He certainly carried those sins to a remote place—all the way to the grave! Second, Jesus is like the sacrificial goat in that He died on our behalf and His blood covers over our sins.

The apostle Paul connected Jesus' sacrifice to the Day of Atonement when he wrote, "God presented Christ as a sacrifice of atonement, through the shedding of his blood." In a very real sense, Jesus is our atonement. He is the one who covers us, and He is the price that was paid for our forgiveness.

What's important is, while the rituals for the Day of Atonement were performed once every year, the sacrifice of Jesus was offered "once for all" (Heb. 7:27). The atonement we receive through Jesus is permanent. Eternal. Again, what a gift!

The Enemy wants you to believe that every time you sin or make a mistake, you are separating yourself from God all over again. He wants you to think you have to keep re-earning God's favor, God's forgiveness.

The truth is that Jesus is the permanent atonement for your sins. When you have Him, nothing else is required.

Response

What are some ways Christians today try to re-earn God's forgiveness over and over again?

What are some ways you can express thanks and praise to Jesus this week?

SCRIPTURE MEMORY

For there is one God and one mediator between God and mankind, the man Christ Jesus, who gave himself as a ransom for all people.

—1 TIMOTHY 2:5-6

DAY 52

Jesus Established a Superior Priesthood

We have this hope as an anchor for the soul, firm and secure. It enters the inner sanctuary behind the curtain, where our forerunner, Jesus, has entered on our behalf. He has become a high priest forever, in the order of Melchizedek.
HEBREWS 6:19-20

In many ways, the Old Testament sacrificial system was unproductive. It also generated very little change. As we've seen, the Jewish people of the ancient world followed a law that required them to offer the same sacrifices year after year, decade after decade, century after century. I imagine that must have felt a little repetitive. Maybe even a little futile.

Actually, it *was* futile. That's because God never intended for the sacrifice of animals by humans to be the solution for our sin problem. Instead, the Old Testament law was designed to help us recognize our sin problem and to help us recognize our inability to solve that problem ourselves. As Paul wrote, "Therefore no one will be declared righteous in God's sight by the works of the law; rather, through the law we become conscious of our sin" (Rom. 3:20).

In reality, the Old Testament system of sacrifice was always meant to be replaced by a new system under a new high priest: Jesus, our Savior.

In Hebrews 6 and 7, scripture explains the transition between the old priesthood, represented by Aaron and his sons, and the new priesthood represented by a mysterious man named Melchizedek. This man was introduced to history all the way back in Genesis 14 as "Melchizedek king of Salem" (v. 18). He appeared to Abraham, who gave him a tithe of all his resources.

Not much else is known about Melchizedek, but we do know that his name means "king of righteousness," and his title (king of Salem) means "king of peace." The author of Hebrews describes him this way: "Without father or mother, without genealogy, without beginning of days or end of life, resembling the Son of God, he remains a priest forever" (7:3). What that means is Melchizedek was a type of Christ. He was a foreshadowing of Jesus.

Then, a little later in history, David wrote a psalm that included a prophecy about the coming Messiah: "The LORD has sworn and will not change his mind: 'You are a priest forever, in the order of Melchizedek'" (110:4). Of course, David was writing about his descendant Jesus, and he declared that Messiah would be a priest not from the tribe of Levi, which was the tribe all priests came from in the Old Testament, but from the order of Melchizedek.

If all that sounds a little complex, it is! We're talking about Jesus both fulfilling the Old Testament priesthood and launching something totally new. But it matters because Jesus meets our needs in ways the old priesthood never could. Jesus is holy and blameless, which means He is separated from the reality of sin. He doesn't need someone above Himself to make atonement for Himself. But more important, it means that Jesus' sacrifice is completely sufficient. For all time, for all people.

In short, Jesus is the High Priest we need. He is superior to every other religious system because He offers everything we need. And He offers it freely and completely. Don't sit on that offer. Don't let the Enemy whisper that it's not enough or that you don't need it, that you don't need Him. You do.

Response

What helps you to see and recognize your need for God?

Why does humanity need Jesus as our High Priest?

SCRIPTURE MEMORY

For there is one God and one mediator between God and mankind, the man Christ Jesus, who gave himself as a ransom for all people.

—1 TIMOTHY 2:5-6

DAY 53

Jesus Established a Superior Covenant

And he took bread, gave thanks and broke it, and gave it to them, saying, "This is my body given for you; do this in remembrance of me."

In the same way, after the supper he took the cup, saying, "This cup is the new covenant in my blood, which is poured out for you."

LUKE 22:19–20

When was the last time you participated in a covenant? If you think the answer is never, you might be surprised. If you've been married, for example, you're part of a covenant. If you've bought a house or a car, you're part of a covenant. If you've made any kind of legal promise or commitment, you're part of a covenant, because that's exactly what a covenant is: an official agreement that is legally binding in some way.

When I started reading through the Bible in a serious way, one of the things that stood out to me was how many covenants there are. In fact, in a lot of ways, the Bible is a string of covenants—binding agreements—between God and humanity.

It started with the flood, when God established a covenant with Noah and his family, promising He would never again destroy the earth through water. Then came what scholars call the Abrahamic covenant, which is actually a series of covenants. In Genesis 15, God promised to give Abraham and his descendants the land of Israel.

In Genesis 17, God established the covenant of circumcision with Abraham and promised that he would be the father of many nations. God described this as an "everlasting covenant" (v. 7).

Next, God extended that covenant by giving the law to Moses— the Ten Commandments and the rest of the laws recorded in Leviticus and Deuteronomy. "Then he took the Book of the Covenant and read it to the people. They responded, 'We will do everything the LORD has said; we will obey'" (Ex. 24:7). Interestingly, this covenant was sealed with blood.

Jump forward a thousand years or so, and God added a covenant with David. God promised that a Savior would come from David's household, saying, "I will establish the throne of his kingdom forever" (2 Sam. 7:13).

Of course, these were all covenants established between God and the Israelites, His chosen people. And of course, since the Israelites were human beings, they constantly violated their end of the bargains. They failed in their promise to be faithful to God, and they suffered many consequences because of that failure.

Then, something totally unexpected happened. Speaking through the prophet Jeremiah, God declared that a "new covenant" was coming. A covenant completely different from the one God established with Abraham and Moses, which humanity had broken. A covenant in which God would write His law not on tablets but on our hearts. A covenant in which "they will all know me, . . . declares the LORD" (Jer. 31:34).

This is the covenant Jesus spoke about during the Last Supper: "This cup is the new covenant in my blood, which is poured out for you." This new covenant includes Jesus as High Priest, which we've seen, and this covenant is superior to the old because it's based entirely on Jesus' death and resurrection. So Jesus carries all the burden of this legal agreement between God and humanity. He carries all the risk.

Which means we carry none.

Response

What are some covenants (legal agreements) you are currently a part of?

What is required for people to participate in this new covenant with Christ?

SCRIPTURE MEMORY

For there is one God and one mediator between God and mankind, the man Christ Jesus, who gave himself as a ransom for all people.

—1 TIMOTHY 2:5-6

DAY 54

Jesus Appointed Us as Priests

But you are a chosen people, a royal priesthood, a holy nation, God's special possession, that you may declare the praises of him who called you out of darkness into his wonderful light. Once you were not a people, but now you are the people of God; once you had not received mercy, but now you have received mercy.

1 PETER 2:9-10

Jaime Maldonado-Aviles spent years working diligently and sacrificing willingly in order to succeed in the world of science. And succeed he did. After studying biology at the University of Puerto Rico, he earned a doctorate at the University of Pittsburgh. Then he devoted six years to a postgraduate program at Yale, walking the cutting edge as an esteemed neuroscientist. Everything was pointing toward a long career filled with accomplishments.

Then Maldonado-Aviles made a decision that surprised everyone, including himself. He left his prestigious career to study for the priesthood. His reason? "This constant intuition—I almost want to say nagging—that maybe I was called to serve in a different way."[1]

Speaking of being surprised, here's something that might surprise you a bit: you are also a priest. It's true! You may not wear a robe or a collar, but if you have a relationship with Jesus Christ, then you are a priest in His kingdom.

177

As we've seen earlier throughout this section, Jesus is the high priest within God's kingdom. He serves as the mediator between God and humanity, and He does so based on a new covenant that both fulfilled and replaced the sacrificial system of the Old Testament. When you put all that together, it means Jesus is the linchpin of our lives— not just our *spiritual* lives, but everything about us. Everything we are and everything we do. It's all based on Christ.

Here's the rub: A lot of people think of Christianity as following Jesus, and there's truth to that. But there's also more. We are called to serve Jesus in His kingdom. And one of the ways we do that is by functioning as His priests.

What does that look like? Well, remember that the priests of the Old Testament offered sacrifices as a way of dealing with the problem of sin. While we don't butcher bulls and sheep, we still offer sacrifices to God—namely, our lives. Paul said, "Therefore, I urge you, brothers and sisters, in view of God's mercy, to offer your bodies as a living sacrifice, holy and pleasing to God—this is your true and proper worship" (Rom. 12:1).

The priests of the Old Testament were also called to lead their community in worshiping God. In a similar way, scripture says all who serve Jesus are a "royal priesthood," "a holy nation." We are "God's special possession, that you may declare the praises of him who called you out of darkness into his wonderful light."

Finally, the priests of the Old Testament represented God to their community. They were ambassadors, liaisons. Likewise, the Bible says, "We are therefore Christ's ambassadors, as though God were making his appeal through us" (2 Cor. 5:20). We are called to serve Jesus by making His name great and by representing Him to all people.

All that is to say you are a priest. So choose to fortify your mind and spend as much time as possible at the table with Jesus so you can serve Him well.

Response

How do you respond to the idea that you are a priest?

In what ways are you currently doing the work of a priest? In what ways are you not?

SCRIPTURE MEMORY

For there is one God and one mediator between God and mankind, the man Christ Jesus, who gave himself as a ransom for all people.

—1 TIMOTHY 2:5-6

Jesus Is Our Redeemer

DAY 55

Jesus Is the Lamb

The next day John saw Jesus coming toward him and said, "Look, the Lamb of God, who takes away the sin of the world! This is the one I meant when I said, 'A man who comes after me has surpassed me because he was before me.' I myself did not know him, but the reason I came baptizing with water was that he might be revealed to Israel."

JOHN 1:29–31

It was an interesting day at the Jordan River. An exciting day. In fact, it was a day that marked a key transition between the old ways and the new.

To back up a little bit, the prophet often referred to as John the Baptist was a wild sort of man by any standard. Like Jesus, John's birth was a miraculous event that included an improbable conception and a visit from the angel Gabriel. Unlike Jesus, lots of people knew about John's birth and the circumstances surrounding it. That's because John was the son of a priest, a known commodity. And the miracles connected to that moment were witnessed by other known commodities in Jerusalem rather than shepherds from the hills of Bethlehem.

Despite his famous beginning, John took a strange turn when he came of age. Rather than follow in his father's footsteps as a priest, John decamped to the wilderness around the Jordan River, about twenty miles east of Jerusalem. Perhaps because of his famous birth, crowds of people began visiting John in the wilderness to hear what he had to say. And John had a lot to say. He preached with fire and passion, urging people to confess their sins and be baptized as a sign of their renewed commitment to God. He often spoke against the hypocritical Pharisees and other religious leaders, calling them a "brood of vipers" (Matt. 3:7).

One day, Jesus came out with the crowds to hear John speak. Jesus even waded into the river, requesting to be baptized. What happened next must have shocked everyone *except* Jesus: "Heaven was opened and the Holy Spirit descended on him in bodily form like a dove. And a voice came from heaven: 'You are my Son, whom I love; with you I am well pleased'" (Luke 3:21–22).

So, yeah, it was an interesting day. What the people didn't understand was that God the Father had just launched the ministry of Jesus, His Son. The same voice that created the universe spoke out to declare that Jesus' mission was in full swing and God was "well pleased."

John understood what was happening, though. He had prepared for this moment his entire life. So when John saw Jesus again, he cried out, "Look, the Lamb of God, who takes away the sin of the world!"

Now, if you and I were standing on the riverbank, we might have felt confused by this declaration. *Lamb of God?* we might have wondered. *Why a lamb? Why not a lion or a bear? Something a little more powerful?*

No. John's wording was perfect. Jesus is the Lamb because He is pure. Unblemished. Innocent. And Jesus is the "Lamb of God" because He came into our world to offer Himself as a sacrifice, to allow His own blood to be shed for you and for me.

Jesus takes away the sin of the world in general, yes, but He takes away your sin specifically. All of it. When you join Him at the table of your heart, you can offer up everything you've ever done that's wrong or shortsighted or violent or sneaky or deceptive or bitter or mean-spirited or egotistical. You can offer everything, and He will take it. And you'll be clean.

Response

What are some other titles or characteristics that apply to Jesus?

How do those titles or characteristics point to Jesus as a lamb?

SCRIPTURE MEMORY

For you know that it was not with perishable things such as silver or gold that you were redeemed from the empty way of life handed down to you from your ancestors, but with the precious blood of Christ, a lamb without blemish or defect.

—1 PETER 1:18–19

DAY 56

Jesus Is the Passover Lamb

On that same night I will pass through Egypt and strike
down every firstborn of both people and animals, and
I will bring judgment on all the gods of Egypt. I am the
LORD. The blood will be a sign for you on the houses where
you are, and when I see the blood, I will pass over you. No
destructive plague will touch you when I strike Egypt.
EXODUS 12:12–13

The Passover may have been the most frightening night in human
history. Not only because people died, and not only because people
faced a mysterious enemy they could not see or touch or resist. No,
the reason that night was so grim and terrible and terrifying is because
God Himself poured out His wrath against an entire nation, and the
consequences were devastating.

For context, the Passover occurred during the time of Moses and
the ten plagues and the Israelites' exodus from Egypt. Moses had been
locked in a battle of wills with Pharaoh, demanding that God's people
be released from slavery. Pharaoh had resisted that demand despite
overwhelming pressure and the undeniable power of God's plagues:
blood, frogs, gnats, flies, dead livestock, boils, hail, locusts, and even
the darkening of the sun.

This night was the final moment in that struggle. God Himself
was coming to Egypt in power, ready to strike the conclusive blow.

Before the strike, however, God sent a warning to His people through Moses. He commanded each household to slaughter a lamb at twilight. "Then they are to take some of the blood and put it on the sides and tops of the doorframes of the houses where they eat the lambs" (Ex. 12:7). God promised to pass over each house that was covered by the blood of the lamb and spare those inside from the terror of death.

What a powerful moment in history and what a powerful example of spiritual foreshadowing. Specifically, the Passover pointed forward thousands of years to the moment when Jesus—the Lamb of God— shed His blood on the cross to cover over the sins of humanity.

It's important to note the Israelites could not sacrifice just any lamb prior to the Passover. They were required to choose an animal "without defect" (v. 5). This meant the animal should be as close to perfect as was possible for a lamb. In the same way, Jesus' sacrifice would not have achieved anything for humanity if He were simply a good person or even a great person. No, He had to be perfect, sinless, for His blood to cover over our transgressions.

Also, notice the sacrifice itself wasn't enough during the Passover. If any of the Israelites in Egypt had simply killed a lamb, they would not have been spared. Instead, they had to take action by applying the blood to their doorposts. In a similar way, we will miss the incredible blessing of Jesus' sacrifice if we don't apply His blood to our lives, if we don't take advantage of the atonement that has been offered.

Jesus is the Lamb of God who takes away not just the sin of the world but our personal sin. Yours and mine. And in doing so, He protects us from spiritual death. That means you don't have to be afraid of the Enemy. Not now and not in that moment when you once and for all step into eternity. You are protected by the blood of Christ.

Response

What does it mean to apply Jesus' blood to our lives?

In what ways do you currently need the protection of Jesus in your life?

SCRIPTURE MEMORY

For you know that it was not with perishable things such as silver or gold that you were redeemed from the empty way of life handed down to you from your ancestors, but with the precious blood of Christ, a lamb without blemish or defect.

—1 PETER 1:18–19

Jesus Suffered on Our Behalf

He was oppressed and afflicted,
 yet he did not open his mouth;
he was led like a lamb to the slaughter,
 and as a sheep before its shearers is silent,
 so he did not open his mouth.
ISAIAH 53:7

I have the privilege of talking with a lot of people about Jesus. Some of those opportunities come about because I'm a pastor, sure. But I also feel a heavy burden for those who have yet to encounter Christ. So, whenever I get a chance to share the good news of the gospel, I take it.

Of course, not everyone wants to hear what I have to say. And if I had to list the different reasons why different people are closed to the gospel message, I think suffering would be near the top. People have a hard time understanding how there can be so much suffering in the world if God exists. They have a tough time accepting how *they* can suffer so much personally if God is good. Suffering is a major stumbling block.

I understand those sentiments. I've had to deal with those questions. But there's one thing we often fail to remember when it comes to this question of suffering—namely, Jesus suffered too. In fact, Jesus suffered in a way no other person in the history of humanity has suffered. And He willingly endured that suffering because of His love for you and me.

Isaiah 53 is a prophecy about the Messiah, and it's one I'm sure must have confused readers in the ancient world for centuries, because it does not describe the Messiah the way most people expected—as a conquering king. Instead, Isaiah 53 reveals how the Christ would be a suffering servant.

"Surely he took up our pain and bore our suffering," Isaiah declared, "yet we considered him punished by God, stricken by him, and afflicted" (v. 4). The prophecy included details that are shocking in their accuracy for those of us with the privilege of hindsight: "But he was pierced for our transgressions, he was crushed for our iniquities; the punishment that brought us peace was on him, and by his wounds we are healed" (v. 5).

There's no doubt Jesus suffered horrendously on the cross. Crucifixion was more about torture than execution, and the Romans were master torturers. But that's not what I'm talking about when I say Jesus suffered more than any other person. I'm talking about His experiences with sin: "We all, like sheep, have gone astray, each of us has turned to our own way; and the LORD has laid on him the iniquity of us all" (v. 6).

On the cross, Jesus willingly bore the entire weight of human sin. Every sin committed by every person in history was thrown upon Jesus in a single moment. And it was agony. He was pierced by the reality of that sin. Crushed by it. And ultimately killed by it.

Led "like a lamb to the slaughter," Jesus chose to suffer so you and I might choose to be blessed. He chose to suffer so that we might have life and have it abundantly. He chose to suffer so we would have the opportunity to fortify our minds and stand firm against the same sin, the same evil He endured.

In short, Jesus suffered to limit your suffering. Because He is the Lamb of God.

Response

What are some primary sources of suffering in your life?

What steps can you take this week to lift up that suffering to Jesus?

SCRIPTURE MEMORY

For you know that it was not with perishable things such as silver or gold that you were redeemed from the empty way of life handed down to you from your ancestors, but with the precious blood of Christ, a lamb without blemish or defect.

—1 PETER 1:18-19

DAY 58

Jesus Is Our Redemption

For you know that it was not with perishable things such as silver or gold that you were redeemed from the empty way of life handed down to you from your ancestors, but with the precious blood of Christ, a lamb without blemish or defect.
1 PETER 1:18–19

What comes to mind when you hear the words *redeem* or *redemption*? Those are church words through and through. Pastors and church leaders use them all the time, and you'll find them all over the place in articles, books, and Bible studies. But what do those terms actually mean?

The answer might surprise you.

Today, we talk about redemption as a synonym for salvation. But that wasn't how the term was used for thousands of years. In fact, in the ancient world, *redeem* and *redemption* weren't spiritual terms at all. They were financial words connected to debt. To redeem something meant to buy it out or buy it back.

Maybe you're wondering, *How did redemption get connected to salvation?* Good question. And the answer has everything to do with Jesus as the Lamb of God.

When the ancient Israelites found themselves in financial difficulty, they had few options. One way to repay a debt was to sell your possessions, but most people in that time didn't have a lot of assets. Besides, credit cards weren't a thing back then, so if people had money to buy stuff, they usually didn't find themselves in financial trouble in the first place.

One way to solve a financial crisis was to sell your land. The other way was to sell yourself, meaning that you voluntarily offered yourself as a servant or slave in order to earn enough money to repay your debt.

As you might imagine, neither option was appealing. In fact, both were deeply shameful in that culture. Therefore, Israelite society allowed for other people, usually family members, to redeem what had been sold—to buy back the land or to buy an individual's freedom.

As we've seen many times in these pages, humanity exists in slavery to sin and death. We are born into that slavery, and we have no way of repaying that sin debt ourselves. We have no way of solving our own problem.

Instead, Jesus solved the problem for us by redeeming us, by buying us out of that debt, not with silver or gold but with His own "precious blood" as the Lamb of God.

Don't miss that. You were in a spiritual dilemma. Your sin had ratcheted up a mighty big bill. It's a spiritual debt, a debt you inherited from Adam, and one you can never pay. So stop trying to pay it! Stop trying to work harder and be good enough. Instead, sit down at the table with Jesus and acknowledge the truth: He paid your debt long ago. He is your redemption.

Response

When did you first realize you were weighed down by the debt of sin and death?

What are specific ways you can express gratitude to Jesus for your redemption?

SCRIPTURE MEMORY

For you know that it was not with perishable things such as silver or gold that you were redeemed from the empty way of life handed down to you from your ancestors, but with the precious blood of Christ, a lamb without blemish or defect.

—1 PETER 1:18-19

DAY 59

Jesus Is Worthy of All Praise

Then I looked and heard the voice of many angels, numbering thousands upon thousands, and ten thousand times ten thousand. They encircled the throne and the living creatures and the elders. In a loud voice they were saying:

> **"Worthy is the Lamb, who was slain,
>   to receive power and wealth and wisdom and strength
>   and honor and glory and praise!"**

REVELATION 5:11–12

Somewhere between sixty and seventy years after the death and resurrection of Jesus Christ, the apostle John received a privilege many in history have longed for: He was shown a vision of heaven. And not just of heaven but of the very throne room of God.

The vision John recorded was electric with majesty and magnificence. He described God as sitting on His throne with "the appearance of jasper and ruby." Behind Him, "A rainbow that shone like an emerald encircled the throne" (Rev. 4:3). There were twenty-four elders surrounding God's throne, each seated on their own smaller throne. From the throne came "flashes of lightning, rumblings and peals of thunder" (v. 5), and in front of that throne "there was what looked like a sea of glass, clear as crystal" (v. 6).

John was dazzled and mesmerized, just as you and I might be if we were to somehow transport a thousand years into the future and try to describe a city advanced well beyond our time.

Continuing the record of his vision, John described four "living creatures" who sounded like nothing on this earth: "The first living creature was like a lion, the second was like an ox, the third had a face like a man, the fourth was like a flying eagle. Each of the four living creatures had six wings and was covered with eyes all around, even under its wings" (vv. 7–8).

Then, in the midst of all that pomp and circumstance, all that power and majesty, John described something new—*someone* new. "Then I saw a Lamb," he wrote, "looking as if it had been slain, standing at the center of the throne, encircled by the four living creatures and the elders. The Lamb had seven horns and seven eyes, which are the seven spirits of God sent out into all the earth" (5:6).

Then the beings in heaven universally bowed to worship this Lamb, this sacrifice that had been slain. The living creatures bowed down. The elders bowed down. Angels numbering ten thousand times ten thousand lifted their voices in praise, declaring, "Worthy is the Lamb, who was slain." They declared the Lamb worthy "to receive power and wealth and wisdom and strength and honor and glory and praise."

This Lamb is Jesus, of course. And it is precisely because He was slain, precisely because He offered Himself as a sacrifice on behalf of all people, that He is worthy of all honor. All glory. All praise.

So praise Him! Right now, right this second. The Lamb of God isn't up in heaven or somewhere in the cosmos far away. He's close. He's with you at the table. So bow, right where you are. Worship. Acknowledge what Jesus offered for you and respond with praise.

Response

What have you been taught about what heaven will be like?

What are specific ways you can give honor, glory, and praise to Jesus this week?

SCRIPTURE MEMORY

For you know that it was not with perishable things such as silver or gold that you were redeemed from the empty way of life handed down to you from your ancestors, but with the precious blood of Christ, a lamb without blemish or defect.

—1 PETER 1:18-19

Jesus Is Worthy to Impose Judgment

You are worthy to take the scroll
and to open its seals,
because you were slain,
and with your blood you purchased for God
persons from every tribe and language and people and
nation.
You have made them to be a kingdom and priests to serve
our God,
and they will reign on the earth.
REVELATION 5:9-10

John began Revelation 5 by describing God as seated on His throne and holding a scroll in His right hand. But this was not just any scroll: "A scroll with writing on both sides and sealed with seven seals" (v. 1). Then John heard an angel cry out in a loud voice, "Who is worthy to break the seals and open the scroll?" (v. 2). The response was silence. Crickets. Nobody in the throne room of heaven was worthy to stand up and take the scroll from God's hand. The tension and dread were apparently so intense that John "wept and wept" (v. 4).

Then came the answer: Jesus, the Lamb of God. "He went and took the scroll from the right hand of him who sat on the throne" (v. 7). That's the moment when all of heaven erupted in praise, when all of heaven glorified Jesus because He alone is worthy to take the scroll and open its seals. Because He was victorious over evil.

Here's the thing, though: that scroll is bad news. As you keep reading in Revelation, you see that each time Jesus broke one of those seven seals, a new horror was released on the earth. The first seal unleashed the Antichrist. The second seal led to brutal warfare. The third seal was famine. The fourth seal was death. And on it goes.

So the question that needs to be answered is this: Why were the residents of heaven overjoyed when the Lamb was found worthy to take the scroll and break the seals? Wouldn't it have been better to keep all that closed?

The answer is all about authority. Specifically, the authority to impose judgment. In the ancient world, a scroll sealed by a king could only be opened by someone with the proper authority, just as top-secret documents today can only be accessed by those who have the necessary security clearance. So the fact that nobody was worthy to break the seals meant nobody had the proper authority to handle what was in the scroll: death, war, famine, pestilence, natural disasters, and so on. Nobody had the authority to judge evil and bring about the end of history.

Then Jesus stepped in. Jesus is worthy to open the scroll because He has authority over all things, including the authority to pronounce judgments against evil. That is wonderful news! Why? Because it means evil and sin do not go unregulated. They are not raging out of control. Instead, it is Jesus, the Lamb of God, who defeated evil and sin through the shedding of His blood. And it is Jesus who has the right and authority to rule as judge.

In short, it is precisely because Jesus has the authority to judge evil that you and I have hope for the future. We know the Lamb has been and will be victorious. Therefore, we can fortify our minds with that truth whenever evil attempts to harm us or distract us in the present.

Response

Why is judgment against evil a good thing?

How should we understand the line between Jesus having authority over all things and Jesus giving people free will to make their own choices?

SCRIPTURE MEMORY

For you know that it was not with perishable things such as silver or gold that you were redeemed from the empty way of life handed down to you from your ancestors, but with the precious blood of Christ, a lamb without blemish or defect.

—1 PETER 1:18-19

Jesus Is the King of Kings

DAY 61

Jesus Is King

Jesus said, "My kingdom is not of this world. If it were, my servants would fight to prevent my arrest by the Jewish leaders. But now my kingdom is from another place."
JOHN 18:36

The twentieth century was not kind to monarchies. In 1900, most of the world was under the control of kings and queens, all of whom demonstrated real power and authority within their realms. But then came World War I. And World War II. And the rise of several powerful political movements, such as democracy, nationalism, Marxism, and more—all of which helped wipe away the majority of those monarchies. Today, there are only around thirty monarchies left. And most of the monarchs currently reigning possess little or no actual power.[1]

Because of this switch in the way our world is run, most people today don't have a lot of experience with kings and queens. Which means many of us find it difficult to truly understand the reality presented in the Bible that Jesus is a king. Really, *the* King.

When Jesus began His public ministry, the very first thing He taught was the reality of what we refer to as the kingdom of heaven or the kingdom of God. "Repent," Jesus said, "for the kingdom of heaven has come near" (Matt. 4:17). That was His first message. That was the primary theme He wanted to communicate: "The kingdom of heaven has come near."

Throughout His ministry, Jesus spent a lot of time describing that kingdom. He told His followers not to waste their time worrying about what they would eat, drink, or wear but to "seek first his kingdom and his righteousness, and all these things will be given to you as well" (6:33). He declared, "The kingdom of heaven is like yeast that a woman took and mixed into about sixty pounds of flour until it worked all through the dough" (13:33). He meant the kingdom has a way of spreading within cultures. It grows. And Jesus taught Nicodemus, the teacher, "Very truly I tell you, no one can see the kingdom of God unless they are born again" (John 3:3).

Jesus also described what it takes to enter the kingdom of heaven. "Not everyone who says to me, 'Lord, Lord,' will enter the kingdom of heaven," He declared, "but only the one who does the will of my Father who is in heaven" (Matt. 7:21). Jesus added, "Truly I tell you, anyone who will not receive the kingdom of God like a little child will never enter it" (Mark 10:15).

Ultimately, Jesus made it clear that the kingdom of God is vastly different from any of the monarchies or nations that have ever existed on earth. It is spiritual. It is heavenly. As He said to Pilate, "My kingdom is not of this world."

We've now spent sixty days exploring the truth of who Jesus is and what He values. He is both God and man. He is our Savior and our Rabbi, our Friend and our Lord. He is both High Priest and the Lamb of God. Jesus is all of these and much, much more.

But the next time you have a conversation with Jesus, remember you are connecting with the King—*your* King. Remember you are building a relationship with the Ruler of the universe. And remember you have that opportunity not because you deserve it but because the King of all things stepped down from His throne and set up a table in the presence of your enemies.

Response

What ideas or images come to mind when you hear the word *king*? Why?

What does it mean on a practical level to say that Jesus is King?

SCRIPTURE MEMORY

In the time of those kings, the God of heaven will set up a kingdom that will never be destroyed, nor will it be left to another people. It will crush all those kingdoms and bring them to an end, but it will itself endure forever.

—DANIEL 2:44

Jesus Is the Eternal King

When your days are over and you rest with your ancestors, I will raise up your offspring to succeed you, your own flesh and blood, and I will establish his kingdom. He is the one who will build a house for my Name, and I will establish the throne of his kingdom forever.
2 SAMUEL 7:12-13

If there's one thing all earthly kings have in common, it's that their reigns don't last forever. From the worst kings in history to the greatest, every single one blazed with limited glory for a little while—some a little longer than others—and then was snuffed out. Extinguished.

Every monarchy that ever existed either has come crashing down or will come crashing down. Sure, many of them were impressive in their day. They left behind palaces and statues, and they left their mark in our history books. But the simple truth is that earthly kingdoms simply do not last.

God's kingdom is different, though, because God's kingdom is eternal. Everlasting. And the same is true for Jesus the King.

In 2 Samuel there's an interesting interaction between King David and God. Having just finished a majestic palace for himself, David felt convicted about where God was hanging out in his kingdom. Specifically, the Israelites were still worshiping God at the tabernacle, which was basically a tent. A large and fancy tent, yes, but still a tent.

So David decided he would build God a house. A temple. He

started making plans. He brought in the best architects and the best designers. He was prepared to spare no expense.

Then God stepped in and told David to stop. God reminded David that He had no need of a dwelling place. He was God! The same being who created galaxies and spun solar systems into existence could not be contained any place on earth, be it a tent, a temple, or the tallest tower.

Instead, God declared He would build David a house—not a physical structure, but a dynasty, a lineage. "When your days are over and you rest with your ancestors," God said, "I will raise up your off-spring to succeed you, your own flesh and blood, and I will establish his kingdom." Then He added, "Your house and your kingdom will endure forever before me; your throne will be established forever" (2 Sam. 7:16).

Of course, God was talking about the Messiah who would be born in the line of David. He was talking about Jesus. But it's important for us to understand that Jesus didn't begin His existence when He was born in Bethlehem a thousand years later. Neither did Jesus suddenly become a king in that moment.

Instead, Jesus has always existed. He is eternal. And He has always existed as the unquestioned ruler of God's kingdom. He has no predecessor. No successor. No heir. He was, is, and always will be King.

The truth is that Jesus set aside His crown and stepped down from His throne so He could accomplish the work only He could accomplish. Salvation. Sacrifice. Redemption. Atonement. All the truths we've explored throughout these pages.

Jesus, the eternal King, did these things so you and I could be part of His kingdom. So reject every voice that tries to whisper in your ear that you are unwanted. Unworthy. Unwelcome. Tell those voices to speak with your King.

Response

Why is it important to remember that Jesus has always existed and always existed as King?

How should Jesus' Kingship influence the way you approach Him and interact with Him?

SCRIPTURE MEMORY

In the time of those kings, the God of heaven
will set up a kingdom that will never be
destroyed, nor will it be left to another people.
It will crush all those kingdoms and bring them
to an end, but it will itself endure forever.

—DANIEL 2:44

Jesus Is King of the Jews

Then the whole assembly rose and led him off to Pilate. And they began to accuse him, saying, "We have found this man subverting our nation. He opposes payment of taxes to Caesar and claims to be Messiah, a king."

So Pilate asked Jesus, "Are you the king of the Jews?"

"You have said so," Jesus replied.

LUKE 23:1-3

It never pays to go toe-to-toe with Jesus. A Roman official, Pontius Pilate, gave it a try after Jesus was arrested, but he came away shaken. In fact, when Pilate finished his interrogation of Jesus, he started a public argument with the chief priests and their mob in Jerusalem, trying to persuade them that Jesus was innocent and should be set free. I'm sure it didn't help when Pilate's wife sent him a note in the middle of his conversation that said, "Don't have anything to do with that innocent man, for I have suffered a great deal today in a dream because of him" (Matt. 27:19).

In the end, Jesus was crucified according to God's plan. But even then Pilate couldn't get past his encounter with Christ. He posted a sign above Jesus' head: JESUS OF NAZARETH, THE KING OF THE JEWS. The religious leaders weren't happy when they saw that sign. "Do not write 'The King of the Jews,'" they protested, "but that this man claimed to be king of the Jews."

Pilate, however, answered, "What I have written, I have written" (John 19:21–22).

Of course, Pilate was thinking of Jesus as *a* king. When he asked Jesus, "Are you the king of the Jews," he meant a small-*K* king. An earthly king. A regional ruler of a little territory called Judea.

Sadly, most of the people in Jesus' day shared Pilate's way of thinking. Even those who followed Jesus believed Him to be a king in the smaller sense of that word. They thought the Messiah would be a second coming of David, or maybe Joshua. They expected the Christ to set up a kingdom on earth, overthrow the Roman Empire, and restore the wealth and power the kingdom of Israel had enjoyed during the days of Solomon.

When Jesus acknowledged His status as King of the Jews, when He told Pilate, "You have said so," He was making a much bigger statement. Specifically, Jesus was claiming to be the fulfillment of the prophecy God declared to David: "He is the one who will build a house for my Name, and I will establish the throne of his kingdom forever. I will be his father, and he will be my son" (2 Sam. 7:13–14).

It's easy for people to try to pigeonhole Jesus according to their own opinions, their own desires. Even today, even within the church, we face the danger of trying to shrink Jesus down to a size that makes us more comfortable.

Jesus is not just a good person or a great moral thinker. Jesus is not a cosmic vending machine or a "get out of jail free" card. He is not a convenient Christ made in our own image.

As you sit across from Him at the table He has prepared for you, worship the King of the Jews in the largest sense of that term. Worship Jesus as your Lord and Master, your Savior, your eternal King.

Response

Where do you see Jesus being minimized in today's culture?

What are appropriate ways to worship Jesus as King?

SCRIPTURE MEMORY

In the time of those kings, the God of heaven
will set up a kingdom that will never be
destroyed, nor will it be left to another people.
It will crush all those kingdoms and bring them
to an end, but it will itself endure forever.

—DANIEL 2:44

DAY 64

Jesus Is the King of Glory

Lift up your heads, you gates;
   lift them up, you ancient doors,
   that the King of glory may come in.
Who is he, this King of glory?
   The LORD Almighty—
   he is the King of glory.

PSALM 24:9-10

My father is an artist, so I've always appreciated art. I imagine how weird it must be to try to paint a picture of Jesus. How would you decide what to paint? How would you go about trying to capture His essence in a meaningful way?

From my experience, it seems most artists who made the attempt chose to focus on what we might call the softer side of the Savior. I'm talking about Jesus as the Good Shepherd, with a sheep draped across His shoulders. Jesus standing at the door and knocking. And, of course, Jesus on the cross.

While those are accurate reflections of specific elements of Christ's character, they don't represent the total package of who Jesus is and what He has accomplished. That's why I'd like to see some modern artists tackle John's description of Jesus in Revelation 1.

When the apostle John was caught up in a vision that included the throne room of heaven, the end of the world, and the glorious city scholars call "the new heaven and the new earth," the very first thing John saw was Jesus. Not Jesus the carpenter, not the softer side of the Savior, but Jesus the King.

"And when I turned I saw seven golden lampstands, and among the lampstands was someone like a son of man, dressed in a robe reaching down to his feet and with a golden sash around his chest." So far, so good, right? I could see an artist painting that. But look at what comes next:

> The hair on his head was white like wool, as white as snow, and his eyes were like blazing fire. His feet were like bronze glowing in a furnace, and his voice was like the sound of rushing waters. In his right hand he held seven stars, and coming out of his mouth was a sharp, double-edged sword. His face was like the sun shining in all its brilliance. (Rev. 1:12–16)

That's Jesus the King! Jesus, who is filled with wisdom and bursting with power. Jesus, whose voice echoes with authority throughout eternity. Jesus the Conqueror and the Judge.

"Who is . . . this King of glory?" David asked. The answer is Jesus as John saw Him. Jesus unveiled. No wonder John said, "When I saw him, I fell at his feet as though dead" (v. 17). Who wouldn't? Who could stand in the face of such a King?

When the Enemy tries to tell you that God can't fix your problem, remember this picture of Jesus. When the Enemy tries to convince you how strong and scary he is, remember how mighty and powerful is your King. And when the Enemy tries to tell you that Christ doesn't care, remember what happened when John struck the floor in terror at the sight of the King of Glory: "Then he placed his right hand on me and said: 'Do not be afraid'" (v. 17).

Response

What picture typically comes to mind when you think of Jesus?

When has Jesus reached out and touched you in a meaningful way?

SCRIPTURE MEMORY

In the time of those kings, the God of heaven
will set up a kingdom that will never be
destroyed, nor will it be left to another people.
It will crush all those kingdoms and bring them
to an end, but it will itself endure forever.

—DANIEL 2:44

DAY 65

Jesus Is King of Kings

The armies of heaven were following him, riding on white horses and dressed in fine linen, white and clean. Coming out of his mouth is a sharp sword with which to strike down the nations. "He will rule them with an iron scepter." He treads the winepress of the fury of the wrath of God Almighty. On his robe and on his thigh he has this name written:

KING OF KINGS AND LORD OF LORDS.

REVELATION 19:14–16

There are two truths about China that I find fascinating. The first is that the Chinese government has been engaged for decades in a systematic campaign to snuff out Christianity within its borders. Laws severely limit the number of churches that can exist in China, Bibles cannot be legally transported into China, and those openly living in China as Christians face increasing levels of persecution, raids, and harassment.

The second truth is that Christianity is exploding in China. Despite the persecution and despite the risks, the church is expanding by leaps and bounds. Protestant Christianity is the fastest growing religion in China (a country that is officially atheist), and many estimates put the total number of Christians in that country at more than 100 million.

How can that be? How can Christianity be thriving in a country where powerful government officials regularly and ruthlessly do everything possible to stamp it out? The answer is Jesus. Specifically, the answer is that Jesus is the King of kings and Lord of lords.

We've been exploring John's vision in the book of Revelation, and one of the key elements of that vision is a final battle between the kingdom of the world—that is, the rulers and powers and authorities of our world—and the kingdom of God.

In that battle, the kingdom of God is led by Jesus, whom John describes in glorious terms:

> I saw heaven standing open and there before me was a white horse, whose rider is called Faithful and True. With justice he judges and wages war. His eyes are like blazing fire, and on his head are many crowns. He has a name written on him that no one knows but he himself. He is dressed in a robe dipped in blood, and his name is the Word of God. . . . On his robe and on his thigh he has this name written: KING OF KINGS AND LORD OF LORDS. (19:11–13, 16).

For thousands of years now, kings and rulers have attempted to strike down and stamp out this idea known as Christianity. The powers of this world have done everything in their power to end the revolution Jesus started, but they have not succeeded. Why? Because Jesus Christ is King of kings and Lord of lords.

For generations into the future, governments and political organizations will try to strike down and stamp out the church. They will try to replace it. Reduce it. Remove it. They will not succeed. Why? Because Jesus Christ is King of kings and Lord of lords.

It's very possible that you may experience religious persecution in your lifetime. You may be attacked for your faith. You may be ridiculed. You may be fired from your job or cancelled by your friends. But those attacks need not prevent you from living the life you were created to enjoy. Why? Because Jesus Christ is King of kings and Lord of lords.

Response

Where do you see our world attempting to snuff out Christian ideas and influence?

In what ways have you been harassed or harmed because of your beliefs about Jesus?

SCRIPTURE MEMORY

In the time of those kings, the God of heaven will set up a kingdom that will never be destroyed, nor will it be left to another people. It will crush all those kingdoms and bring them to an end, but it will itself endure forever.

—DANIEL 2:44

Jesus Is the Victorious King

And I heard a loud voice from the throne saying, "Look! God's dwelling place is now among the people, and he will dwell with them. They will be his people, and God himself will be with them and be their God. 'He will wipe every tear from their eyes. There will be no more death' or mourning or crying or pain, for the old order of things has passed away."
REVELATION 21:3-4

Watching live sports can be intense. I live in the South, and I know plenty of people (like me) who get really fired up for their favorite teams (Auburn), especially when it comes to college football. These are people who attend games, buy jerseys, stay up-to-date on all the latest news and all the potential matchups. They are serious! And when they watch a game live, they just might experience some severe stress.

But what if those same fans were to rewatch a game they'd already seen? What if they watched a recording of a game knowing their team had already won? That would be a zero-stress experience, right? When the other team scores a touchdown, my friends would just smile. Maybe offer a little golf clap. Even if the other team built up a substantial lead, my friends wouldn't be bothered at all because they already know the outcome. They know they're on the winning team.

Incredibly, we can have that same experience as followers of Jesus, as servants of the King. Because no matter what happens in our lives and no matter what the future may bring, we know we're on the winning team. We know our King is victorious.

Taken as a whole, the story of the Bible is a story of victory. In the beginning, everything God created was good, including the human race. But then sin entered the picture, and with it came evil. Corruption. Death. Separation from God.

For centuries upon centuries, we have been in rebellion against God and His kingdom. Yes, that rebellion has largely been led by Satan and the forces of evil, but we can't hold ourselves apart. We can't hold ourselves blameless. The truth is we have participated in that rebellion every time we've said no to God's will and yes to our own, every time we chose to be lords over our own lives. Little-*K* kings choosing to serve ourselves rather than serve our King.

Yet for centuries upon centuries, God has been working to restore what was lost and to fix what was broken. He has been following His plan to conquer evil once and for all and repair the relationship between Himself and humanity.

The final chapters of Revelation show us the end of that plan. They show us the victory of our King. Satan defeated. Death itself defeated. In its place, a new heaven and a new earth where "God's dwelling place is now among the people, and he will dwell with them." No more tears. No more pain. Instead, a wedding between Christ and His church—our relationship restored. Instead, a return to Eden where "the leaves of the tree are for the healing of the nations" (22:2) and where "no longer will there be any curse" (v. 3). Where we will see our King face to face.

That's the end of the story. That's the end of *your* story. So remember that reality as you sit with your Savior at the table. Soak in that victory. Saturate yourself in that truth.

Jesus has won. Your King is victorious. And you are already reaping the benefits.

Response

What have you learned about Jesus throughout these pages?

How will that knowledge help strengthen your faith and fortify your mind?

SCRIPTURE MEMORY

In the time of those kings, the God of heaven
will set up a kingdom that will never be
destroyed, nor will it be left to another people.
It will crush all those kingdoms and bring them
to an end, but it will itself endure forever.

—DANIEL 2:44

Notes

Introduction

1. Rita Reif, "Most Expensive Table," *New York Times*, February 2, 1990, https://www.nytimes.com/1990/02/02/arts/auctions.html.

Day 1: Jesus Is God

1. Harriet Tubman quoted in Robert C. Plumb, *The Better Angels: Five Women Who Changed Civil War America* (Lincoln, NE: University of Nebraska Press, 2020).

Day 3: Jesus Is the Word of God

1. Staff Writer, "How Many Copies of the Bible Are Sold Each Year?" Reference, April 3, 2020, https://www.reference.com/world-view /many-copies-bible-sold-year-3a42fbe0f6956bb2.

Day 4: Jesus Created Everything

1. David J. Eicher, "How Many Galaxies Are There? Astronomers Are Revealing the Enormity of the Universe," *Discover*, May 19, 2020, https://www.discovermagazine.com/the-sciences/how-many-galaxies -are-there-astronomers-are-revealing-the-enormity-of-the.

Day 5: Jesus Created You

1. Amit Agarwal, "Visualizing a Trillion: Just How Big That Number Is?" Digital Inspiration, March 3, 2009, https://www.labnol.org /internet/visualize-numbers-how-big-is-trillion-dollars/7814/.

Day 10: Jesus Is a Historical Person

1. Tacitus, Annals XV.44, quoted in Lawrence Mykytiuk, "Did Jesus Exist? Searching for Evidence Beyond the Bible," *Biblical Archaeology Review*, January/February 2015, https://www.biblicalarchaeology.org /daily/people-cultures-in-the-bible/jesus-historical-jesus/did-jesus-exist/.

Day 16: Jesus Saves Us from Evil

1. Christian Oord, "Believe It or Not: Since Its Birth the USA Has Only Had 17 Years of Peace," War History Online, May 19, 2019, https:// www.warhistoryonline.com/instant-articles/usa-only-17-years-of -peace.html.

Day 17: Jesus Saves Us from Death

1. John Donne, "Death Be Not Proud," Poetry Foundation, https://www .poetryfoundation.org/poems/44107/holy-sonnets-death-be-not-proud.

Day 21: Jesus Taught Us How to Pray

1. "Longest Telephone/Video Conversation (Team of Two)," Guinness World Records, https://www.guinnessworldrecords.com/world-records /longest-telephonevideo-conversation-(team-of-two).

Day 22: Jesus Taught About False Teachers

1. Jonathan Romeo, "Following GPS Route, 30-foot Box Truck Becomes Stuck on Engineer Pass," *Durango Herald*, October 19, 2020, https:// durangoherald.com/articles/350732.

Day 28: Jesus Is the Good Shepherd

1. Sam Knight, "The Tweeting of the Lambs: A Day in the Life of a Modern Shepherd," *New Yorker*, April 27, 2018, https://www.newyorker .com/news/letter-from-the-uk/the-tweeting-of-the-lambs-a-day-in-the -life-of-a-modern-shepherd; James Rebanks, *The Shepherd's Life: Modern Dispatches from an Ancient Landscape* (New York: Flatiron Books, 2015).

Day 29: Jesus Is the Resurrection and the Life

1. Associated Press, "Man Attends His Own Funeral in Brazil," CBS News, November 4, 2009, https://www.cbsnews.com/news/man -attends-his-own-funeral-in-brazil/.

Day 32: Jesus Is Lord over Creation

1. "Titanic's Unsinkable Stoker," BBC News, March 20, 2012, https:// www.bbc.com/news/uk-northern-ireland-17543632.

Day 37: Jesus Is Your Friend

1. "Best Friends for 60 Years Discover They Are Brothers," CBS News, December 26, 2017, https://www.cbsnews.com/news/best-friends-for -60-years-discover-they-are-brothers/.

Day 38: Jesus Loves You

1. Hal David and Burt Bacharach, "What the World Needs Now Is Love," © New Hidden Valley Music Co., Casa David Music, 1965.

Day 39: Jesus Offers You Grace

1. John Newton, "Amazing Grace," 1779.

Day 43: Jesus Is Head of the Church

1. "The Oldest Churches in the World," Oldest.org, https://www.oldest .org/religion/churches/.

Day 46: Jesus Unites the Church as His Body

1. Sarah Gibbens, "New Human 'Organ' Was Hiding in Plain Sight," *National Geographic*, March 27, 2018, https://www. nationalgeographic.com/news/2018/03/interstitium-fluid-cells-organ -found-cancer-spd/.

2. Stephanie Pappas, "Scientists Discover New Organ in the Throat," LiveScience, October 20, 2020, https://www.livescience.com/new -salivary-gland.html.

Day 48: Jesus Preserves His Church

1. Jiachuan Wu, Daniel Arkin, and Robin Muccari, "An Icon in Flames," NBC News, April 2019, https://www.nbcnews.com/news/world/notre -dame-fire-what-was-damaged-n995371.

Day 54: Jesus Appointed Us as Priests

1. Julie Zauzmer, "Why a Yale Neuroscientist Decided to Change Careers—and Is Now Becoming a Priest," *Washington Post*, March 3, 2017, https://www.washingtonpost.com/news/acts-of-faith/wp/2017 /03/03/why-a-yale-neuroscientist-decided-to-change-careers-and-is -now-becoming-a-priest/.

Day 61: Jesus Is King

1. Staff, "How the World's Monarchs Are Adapting to Modern Times," *The Week*, June 16, 2019, https://theweek.com/articles/847076/how -worlds-monarchs-are-adapting-modern-times.

About the Author

Louie Giglio is pastor of Passion City Church and the original visionary of the Passion movement, which exists to call a generation to leverage their lives for the fame of Jesus.

Since 1997, Passion Conferences has gathered college-aged young people in events across the United States and around the world. Most recently, Passion hosted over 700,000 people from over 150 countries online at Passion 2021.

Louie is the national-bestselling author of over a dozen books, including his newest release, *Don't Give the Enemy a Seat at Your Table*, as well as *Goliath Must Fall, Indescribable: 100 Devotions About God and Science, The Comeback, The Air I Breathe, I Am Not but I Know I Am,* and others. As a communicator, Louie is widely known for messages such as "Indescribable" and "How Great Is Our God."

An Atlanta native and graduate of Georgia State University, Louie has done postgraduate work at Baylor University and holds a master's degree from Southwestern Baptist Theological Seminary. Louie and his wife, Shelley, make their home in Atlanta.